# DATING THE WRONG MEN

by Kelly Rossi

illustrations by Stephanie Olivieri

Dating the Wrong Men by Kelly Rossi

Social Magnitude LLC
Las Vegas, NV 89118

Printed in the United States of America

© 2014 by Kelly Rossi
Artwork © 2014 by Stephanie Olivieri

Edition ISBNs
        Softcover: 978-0-9906514-0-6
        eBook: 978-0-9906514-1-3
        PDF: 978-0-9906514-2-0

10 9 8 7 6 5 4 3 2 1

Disclaimer: This publication is sold with the understanding that the author is not engaged in rendering psychological, medical, or other professional services. If expert assistance or counseling is needed, the services of a competent professional should be sought.

This book is based on true events. The author has tried to recreate events, locales and conversations from memories of them. In order to maintain their anonymity in some instances names and identifying details have been changed.

# Dedicated To:

Every girl who has sat, wondering
"Why hasn't he called?"
&
The "Right Men" who know how to
behave to not end up in this book.

# Table of Contents

# The Geek in Disguise

BY JOHN RUSSO
Co-author of Night of the Living Dead

Kelly Rossi is a bright, clever, personable young woman, easy on the eyes and easy to talk to if she's sure you understand and appreciate her wit and intelligence. She does not suffer fools gladly. When I first met her, at a convention called Scarefest in Lexington, Kentucky, I was amused by the business card she handed me, showing that she's the webmaster for the Maloof Skateboarding Company and displaying her facetious self-chosen moniker: "The Geek in Disguise." Smitten by her good looks and her wry sense of humor, I promptly acknowledged that it was "the best geek disguise I'd ever seen!" We both laughed. Then we enjoyed comparing notes about the zany, offbeat, slightly shady characters that populate our Italian heritage.

Each year, as the co-creator of NIGHT OF THE LIVING DEAD and the writer/producer/director of a string of terror-suspense novels and horror movies, I appear as a featured guest at quite a few horror conventions, and Scarefest will always rank as one of my favorites because it was where I met Kelly, who was there promoting her friend and his hit TV show, Ghost Adventures.

The three of us had a lot of fun that night, attending a party honoring George Romero, and then getting to know each other over cocktails, running gags, off-color jokes and interesting conversation. It was a kick to discover that Kelly and I are on the same wavelength about a lot of things, and that we share an unabashed zest for the good things in life spiced up with a ribald sense of humor.

Kelly and I kept in touch by email and by phone after that, and I was greatly amused by her flippant blogs about men and dating that she posts on the Internet. Her blogs are witty, honest and self-revelatory -- as charming as they are daring. I suggested that she should write a book. And now, to my great satisfaction, she has done so.

DATING THE WRONG MEN is written boldly in her own inimitable style, and I assure you that it is unfailingly entertaining and enlightening -- a true guide to love and romance for women working their way through the murky world of personal relationships. It tells all about Kelly's adventures and misadventures on her way to realizing her dreams. It doesn't pull any punches, but unsparingly explores her struggles to understand herself and what's best for her, even as she fights against the machinations and manipulations foisted upon her by others.

I often have said that it's almost a hazard to be a woman in today's selfish, male-ego-driven society, and what Kelly has gone through certainly tends to prove that. But it also shows that an indomitable spirit and an emerging sense of self-worth can overcome bad experiences that may stretch all the way back to early childhood.

This is your chance to let Kelly show you how you can conquer your own demons -- even the ones who may be sleeping alongside you.

# Preface and Acknowledgements

I've gone back and forth while writing this book trying to figure out if my experience dating is common these days, or if I was just one of the lucky ones who found herself in the most bizarre dating circumstances at every turn. Feedback has shown me that Dating the Wrong Men is standard today. But, being the over-achiever I am, I just took it to the extreme. At first, living out these stories was difficult and some harder than others. But I found as I accepted that Dating the Wrong Men was just part of my life, the easier the experiences came as I removed any expectations of a 'normal' dating life. During my single days, it got to the point where my friends couldn't wait to hear what my latest story was because it was inevitably going to be shocking, hilarious or both. There are only so many times that people can tell you "You need to write a book" before you actually do it. So I have.

There are a lot of people to thank for the creation of this book and for their help through the years of these stories.

First, I have to thank God for this crazy life he's given me and the ability to always see things positively. I guess it was a major hint when he gave me the B positive blood type.

Secondly, I need to thank my mom. As you'll see from the story, our relationship came a long way through the years and even longer through the creation of the book. Her shock of first reading the book turned into being one of the most helpful hands in the creation as she made the final edits. I love you Mom and I'm proud of how close our relationship is now.

Thank you to my Right Man, Dale. Thank you for encouraging the story I had to write. You are the reason women are reading this book. You are proof that a woman can go through hell and back and still have hope of finding that one man who makes perfect sense to them, who will love them in all the ways they have been looking for.

Thank you to the man, the myth, the legend John Russo. Encouraging creative writing is one thing, but helping me edit and publish this book is above and beyond any help I've ever got on a project. The words Thank You can't cover my gratitude. But hopefully, you now have some more character material for your next horror script.

Thank you to my illustrator Stephanie Olivieri and her amazing creativity in turning the "Wrong Men" of this book into cartoons.

Thank you to the Wrong Men. There are two sides to every story and this book is written from your Wrong Girl's perspective. In every situation, there were good times and there were bad, but hopefully this book reflects the positive lessons that came from them all.

Finally, thank you to all my close girlfriends who were all going through this at the same time. You'll find all too familiar references in these pages. Thank you for the support, the ladies nights, the cocktails, the late night phone calls and of course all the adventures on our way to find the Right Man!

Cheers!

| | | |
|---|---|---|
| Alexis | Kira | Nicole |
| Ali | Krista | Ruby |
| Anna | Kristin | Shayna |
| Courtney | Laura | Sugar |
| Dana | Leslie | Susan |
| Heather | Lindsey | Teresa |
| Hilary | Michelle | Traci |
| Joey | Misty | Vicki |
| Karen | Morgan | |

# Introduction

From an early age, little girls are taught through fairy tales that their perfect, handsome, loyal, and independently wealthy prince will magically come to them with no effort on their part at all. However, I have yet to meet a girl who sat around in a tower dropping her hair out the window until the man of her dreams climbs up. I have never known of a girl expelled by her stepmother to live in the forest where, lo and behold, a prince is waiting along with seven smaller than average personal assistants await with curiously large ranges of emotion. And on the most extreme side of unbelievable stories, the day has yet to come when we find a woman sleeping her entire life away and still scoring the "fairest of them all". When the day comes for us to hang up our tiaras and princess dress-up clothes for real life, we're all in for a rude awakening. Our parents aren't Kings or Queens, the ratio of frogs to princes in this world has been greatly underestimated and the man of your dreams is more likely to show up looking like Jack Sparrow instead of a valiant prince.

Many people have told me, "You definitely haven't been afraid to live life!" And that's one of the best compliments I can get. I've had the most amazing experiences. I've achieved success in business working with celebrities throughout the world, and I haven't stopped yet! As a complete computer junky nicknamed the Geek In Disguise, I like to tell people, "If you can't find me online, your computer is broken." I have a truly loving relationship that fits me perfectly. But it hasn't always been this way.

This isn't another book by an overly confident man psycho-analyzing everything you're doing wrong, giving you that supposed 'turn-key' answer he's created because it was the exact formula that was worked on him by his wife. I've read those books, and all that ever did was make me second guess every single action I took in a relationship. This also isn't some story about Sally Sue's path to love who grew up in a picture perfect family with positivity, encouragement and flowers falling at her every step. This is a story of a situation, so similar to what most people in the world are faced with today. Women and men who come from broken situations, searching through the sea of broken individuals, hoping for that perfect match that will seal their life into solidity and understanding. This is a love story for anyone who's caught herself overanalyzing, making excuses, giving second chances, interpreting text messages, waiting for someone special or even swearing off love forever. This is a story of a girl who has dated every wrong man in existence and not only lived to tell the tale, but did it without bitterness and found the love of her life in the process. And although I've never been given credentials technically, using Malcom Gladwell's 10,000 Hour Rule to success (which states that the key to success in any field is to practice that task for 10,000 hours) you will find from this book that I have been successful 500 times over when it comes to dating the Wrong Men.

Although most parents aim to create a solid framework for their child's future in life and love, sometimes who they are, their situations in life and society as a whole backfire, leaving an entire generation lost. I mean, what did we think would happen with the generation spawned in the 80's, a decade of not knowing the consequences of much of anything? One of the most un-thought-out trends of the 80's was that of the "Latch-key Kid," where kids all over the country were equipped with a house key hanging around their necks and sent on their way. With the decade of sex, drugs, Rock n Roll, aerosol hair sprayed foot-high bangs, and OZZY Osborne biting the heads off bats, I'm surprised more 5 year olds weren't hooked up to car keys to make their way to their store to buy their pregnant mom some more smokes. Although I didn't have those car keys and my mother was smoke-free, "Latch-key Kid" was the approach my parents adopted with me. I didn't have much time with my father when I was young, due to his demanding engineering job. He had a heavily sarcastic sense of humor, which is great when you grow up with the similar traits and sit down to write about your dating experiences. However, as a child I would always be left confused thinking the punchline was me. My mother was set on a mission to prove to her two young daughters that women could be independent and have a careers of their own. As important as that lesson was, it left much of my childhood figuring things out on my own.

An example of my role in the family is when I attempted to climb a shelving unit around the age of four, only to have the entire thing come crashing down on me on the cement. Following standard procedure in my family, my broken rib was completely ignored and I was told to "stop whining". Even then, my approach to life reflected what was to become of my approach to my dating life. I would do something stupid. Those claiming to be close to me ignored, or didn't realize, any real damage I'd done to myself and I'd find a way to get through it all with a smile on my face and as the only person I knew with five pack abs.

My parents' relationship with each other was what I call their "staying roommates", not even giving the faint trace of a loving relationship, "for the sake of the kids." This strategy left me on my own to figure out how to get through life and somehow find a healthy relationship.

Despite my parents' absence and shining example of their loveless marriage, they provided what they thought was right at the time and gave me many tools which made me the person I am today. Both of my parents were brilliant. They made sure I was in a ridiculous amount of extra-curricular activities. I later found out that I had begged to be in at least one extracurricular activity per night of the week to occupy my ridiculously high energy levels. I'm glad I did that since, otherwise, it would have resulted in wearing circles into the lawn due to me running around like crazy. However, it was always being involved in sports, music, art that gave me versatility. My parents also always made sure I had a great education. I didn't have a clue about the important aspects of relationships, but I had the tools to learn by trial and error and that is exactly what I have done.

When I was headed off to college, my parents divorced, and I was shipped the remainder of my belongings from the house. My father remained consumed by work. My mother moved off the continent having landed her dream job as a librarian at military stations all over the world and I was headed off on my misdirected path with no map.

What's crazy is that this parental approach was completely typical of society at the time. Our standards in society have diminished as TV families have moved from the Cleavers to the Bundy's to the over indulgent, child exploiting, paternity questioning family of Honey Boo Boo. We went from honoring men who were good fathers, workers and husbands to idolizing disrespectful men with multiple girlfriends and abusive behavior. Then, we reward them with multi-million dollar recording deals, sports contracts and reality TV shows. To top it off, instead of teaching their sons how to treat a woman, some single moms, picking up the pieces of their own broken relationships, spoil their little boys, turned them into the "Man of the House" and tell everyone, including themselves, that their "baby can do no wrong." Well guess what? Your baby is full of wrong now! This has left a dating pool filled with "Wrong Men" that women of all ages have to swim through, hopelessly wondering if any of it is worth their time. Seeing the damage that has been done only makes me scared for the days when the little girls who get knocked up for the sole purpose of keeping their boyfriend or to land a show on MTV raise boys who start dating.

> This has left a dating pool filled with "Wrong Men" that women of all ages have to swim through.

On the other end of the spectrum, one of the most famous women of our time is a girl became famous because she made a sex tape. This is now the standard some women are trying to achieve. The controlling "I'll slash your tires if you don't do what I want or give me money" kind of girls running around sleeping with everyone in the dating pool hasn't made things easier! Rational women are hit right out of the gates by guys with phrases like "All girls are crazy, I'm just waiting to see what happens from dating you." Then, when they realize the lack of complete insanity in their lives, men figure that you must not be that into them so they move on to more dysfunctional pastures. Friends of mine have also suggested that the millennial generation, ironically called the "Me" generation at one point, came in and made a fad of unethical decisions and taking no responsibility for their own behavior. Obviously all of these factors add even more complexity to the hope of finding that healthy relationship.

This brings me to why I'm writing this book. Let's face it, it's unlikely that the first man you meet will sweep you off your feet, saving you from a lifetime of dating hell let alone offer to pay for dinner. And not everyone has Dr. Phil on speed dial to show you how to get through messes in your dating life. If you have a great support system of friends and family, you might have an easier time dealing with the Wrong Men that show up in your life. Even then, you might still get a rotten apple that no one sees coming. However, if you have an upbringing remotely similar to mine, you'll have no choice but to either learn from others or from your own mistakes. Since I have taken the liberty of doing the latter and dating every type of wrong man in existence, I've decided to share it with you and hopefully it will save you from trying this path on your own.

# The Wrong Men

The "Wrong Men" in my stories aren't necessarily the updatable scum of the earth that I picked up on the side of the road with a sign that read "Will Date For Food". Most either were on their own paths of trial and error through life that would result in the massive destruction of our relationship, or sometimes we just didn't match up to each other in one way or another. Some of the guys who had qualities that I felt were show stoppers turned around to find a woman who never thought twice about the exact reason he and I didn't work out.

Although every girl friend I had through my single years told me "I just can't figure out your 'type'," almost all the wrong men in my stories had a few common positive attributes. I have always dated guys who were handsome, and every man I've dated has been intelligent. However, this does not mean they made intelligent decisions. To hold true to covering all the types of wrong men, you'll see a wide variety of stories that I've lived. Some are unbelievable, some sad, some hilarious, and some will have you dedicating your life to improving the education system in the country.

As you'll see, through the stories and through the years, dating the wrong men changed my standards. It opened my eyes to who I was and what I deserved despite the lack of anyone being there on a regular basis who could explain this to me. I was led through dating hell to finally be able to live the wonderful life that I have today, with an appreciation that can only come from seeing the worst. I can only hope that my stories can help to guide at least one fabulous girl out of the hopeless spot she is in to a place where she can realize that she is worth all the love and respect in the world from her own personal Mr. Right.

# The Abusive Control Freak

Whether it's from obsession with fast cars, an addiction to alcohol or a raging libido, adolescents generally lose control of everything! And it's all part of the job of growing up, even though some never do. As we develop in our schooling, friendships, and careers, we pull ourselves together enough to at least appear to know what we're doing. But every once in a while, we might come across a "Wrong Man" who could care less about his appearance and has his control panel set to overdrive.

Three times in my life, I met a man I knew was "Meant to Be." The first time, I was about 5 years old when I met a son of one of my father's employees. Although we were just little kids swimming in the pool and creating forts out of card board boxes, somehow, I knew this kid was going to be my first love. At that age, it wasn't like I was running on the beach open-armed towards some Jake Gillenhaul-looking stud. It was more like a little brat throwing footballs at my face. But I knew all the same he would be "the one." Maybe I should have interpreted that bombardment of footballs aimed at my head and seen what was coming.

> Those weren't really butterflies in my stomach, but moths that were confused as if someone had turned out the light.

Both of our families were transferred to Oregon because of our father's jobs. Through the awkward early-teen years of my glasses, perms and high water jeans, I dated a few guys, but I knew the day would come when I'd meet up with my childhood crush. Eleven years after we met, we got together. For the first time in my life, I felt like I found someone I could share anything with. At first, I was absolutely enamored about the fact that we would do everything together whether it was partying, sneaking away on camping trips, or going to Grateful Dead shows. I was so excited about this guy that I didn't even realize that those weren't really butterflies in my stomach, but moths that were confused as if someone had turned out the light. He was an extremely good dramatic actor which seemed impressive at first. But, when our day-to-day life started turning into what appeared to be his next scene on his delusional self-occupied stage of life, I learned a lot more about that "Meant to Be" feeling. I was so blindly in love that I kept making excuses for the ever-deteriorating way he treated me.

My first love was also my first, but definitely not last, introduction to "other women." One day after school my girlfriend and I were in the bathroom together doing our hair. She seemed very anxious about something and finally spit it out. A friend of hers had called her and told her she slept with my first love while I was out of town. Completely shocked, I said "Oh, well, I kissed someone else too." Thinking about how some guy kissed my face while I was visiting colleges as I pushed him away stating I had a boyfriend. Hardly the entangled moment that apparently my guy was having in a hot tub back home. When my friend left, I confronted him. I wanted to end it, but something inside me badly wanted that closeness I thought we had. That yearning to feel loved lead me to believe one of his best dramatic acting performances where in which he explained through copious tears how blacked-out drunk and sorry he was. Years later, he would start talking about this night with unsparing details. Now, I am no doctor, but I would diagnose this as a very convenient amnesia.

Any action or hint of a loving relationship started being replaced by anger, threats, and manipulations greatly influenced by his theatrical background. I was constantly altering my personality to fit into what he wanted. I thought, "Well, this is my 'true love.' He won't hurt me, he has my best interest in mind. Because that is love. La la la." as he manipulated me away from all the things I loved in life and the friendships I had. I was completely lost, completely controlled, and no longer happy. If I stood up for myself, the self-obsessed actor would throw a dramatic scene that would include everything from screaming insults to throwing objects. Not knowing my options, I gave in to him and gave up on me. One night, I brought up one of the millions of things that had been eating away at my soul only to have him drape a blanket around himself like a cape, exit stage right (the front door), and lie down in the middle of the common area of our apartment complex, faking a convulsion. I don't remember hearing a standing ovation, but he did get what he wanted, and I gave up.

It finally hit me one day that my life had become a series of actions to avoid another blow up. I was living in fear. It was hard to abandon the false dream that I had found a loving person in my life, but I decided getting out of this relationship would end the dismal play that I never even tried out for. Of course, I was wrong. The break-up apparently was the climax to his screenplay where the main character, himself, would lose his mind completely. In a response to his begging to stay in each other's lives, I agreed to try to "stay friends." In my head, staying friends meant having respect for someone I had dated. In his, it meant stalking, constant harassment and further abuse.

When most people go to college, their days are filled with trying to stay awake through classes, keg stands, and tailgating. My college days might as well have included Michael Meyers lurking in the bushes in a complete horror story. Nights would pass with me sitting on my bed in my new studio apartment, scared out of my mind, on the phone with the cops because my crazy ex was beating the door down. His newest activities included following me everywhere I went, stealing my car, intercepting at my front door any man I tried to date, breaking into my house to steal my birth control pills and leave notes everywhere saying "Don't get pregnant" and printing out massive quantities of pictures of me naked and threatening to spread them through the campus. As an excuse to come see me on a regular basis, he gave me his dog saying he couldn't take care of it anymore.

After about a year of these tactics, he worked himself up to his grand finale. He called me and asked me to pick up some of my things at his house. When I arrived, he had downed an entire bottle of pills and was passed out at the computer. I noticed on the screen that he was writing the screenplay of our relationship. I suddenly realized that every psychotic attempt to ruin my life was part of a demented attempt to get new content for a play. I called a friend and we rushed him to the medical hospital. Doctors took hours pumping his stomach and gave him drugs to counteract whatever he took. Then I was given specific instructions. I was told to bring him to his house, but take away any drug or alcoholic substance from the premises. According to doctor's orders, I cleared out his house. I was loading some bottles of wine into my car when he came chasing after me, grabbing my neck choking me as hard as he could. Our friend broke him off of me and I left as fast as I could. I spent nights in a hotel room so he couldn't find me until the cops issued me a restraining order. Finally, most of the insanity stopped. However, at one point the dog he gave me mysteriously disappeared from my back yard only to end up back at his house.

I learned a lot in this "first love" relationship...

1. This fiasco was not true love. I heard Dr. Phil once say to a man that he needed to guide his daughters and show them the high standard of how they need to be treated or they will allow the first boy who shows them any attention to treat them like crap. This is exactly what happened to me.

2. If someone you think you're in love with will go to extremes to get away from taking care of your needs, the only spotlight they see in the relationship is the one on themselves.

3. Making a clean cut when ending the relationship can be the best decision of your life.

4. If I could get through this mess in a relationship, I could get through anything.

5. Never allow a man to take a picture of you naked! Thank God this was way before social media sites took off because online is forever!

# Signs You Are Dating an Abusive Control Freak:

- If you don't know what constitutes physical abuse, go to a Krav Maga class for a day. Anything done there should not be accepted in a relationship… unless you have that whole dominatrix thing going on. Even then, use a safe word.

- A Past of Violence with Their Friends/Family/Past Relationships.

- Dramatic Scenes – With or without Screenplay.

- Constant criticism of you, your friends, your hobbies, or anything else that makes you happy.

- Everything revolves around him and suddenly there is no more time for what you want to do in life.

- Questioning your every move.

- Holes in the bedroom walls.

- They're telling you what you can and cannot do.

I know while going through an abusive situation, you're being manipulated into thinking things are better than they are. A wise counselor introduced to me the cycle of violence[1]. If you recognize the patterns here, it's time to embrace your intuition and move to a healthy place.

## THE HONEYMOON

**ABUSER'S ACTIONS**
• Begs for forgiveness
• Apologizes, cries
• Goes to NA or AA
• Sends presents and flowers to convince victim to return
• Feels remorse

**VICTIM'S RESPONSE**
• Agrees to stay, return, or take abuser back
• Attempts to stop legal proceedings
• Sets up counseling
• Feels happy & hopeful

**ABUSER'S ACTIONS**
• Is moody
• Isolates Victim
• Withdraws affection
• Yells
• Drinks / Does Drugs
• Threatens
• Criticizes
• Is sullen
• Tension Builds

## TENSION

**VICTIM'S RESPONSE**
• Attempts to calm abuser
• Nurturing
• Silent / Talkative
• Keeps children quiet
• Stays away from family and friends
• Agrees
• Tries to Reason
• Cooks abuser's favorite food
• Has general feeling of "Walking on eggshells"

**The Cycle of Violence**

**ABUSER'S ACTIONS**
• Physically, sexually and/or emotionally abuses victim
• Controls and wields power

**VICTIM'S RESPONSE**
• Protects self in any way
• Police called by you, children, or neighbor
• Tries to calm abuser
• Tries to reason
• Leaves
• Fights back

## VIOLENCE

The more times the cycle is completed the less time it takes to complete.
As the cycle is repeated, the violence usually increases in frequency and severity.

---

[1] The cycle of abuse is a social cycle theory developed in 1979 by Lenore E. Walker. This graphic is one interpretation of it. - Walker, Lenore E. (1979) The Battered Woman. New York: Harper and Row.

## Final Thoughts on an Abusive Control Freak

Emotional, psychological, sexual, and physical - there are many types of abuse. If you're in situation with a man who treats you as though it's his way or the highway, it's time to start packing your car. After hearing stories about girls going ballistic, going after their men with knives, biting, trashing their houses, then running to the cops with some ridiculous lie about how their men had abused them, I was very hesitant to go to the police. But, if you're in a situation where you're dealing with a man who commits or even threatens abuse, go to the cops. That's what they're there for and if it's a day too late you may not have the option.☐

In any kind of abusive situation, help is not far away. From removing yourself, finding a safe place, to rebuilding your life, look into the resources here and the many more you can find online if you're in an abusive situation trying to get back on a healthy path. Your state or city probably also has additional resources.

## Women's Crisis Resources:

National Coalition Against Domestic Violence:
    NCADV.org
    1-800-799-SAFE (7233)

Women Helping Battered Women
    WHBW.org
    1-800-ABUSE95

The National Domestic Violence Hotline
    TheHotline.org
    1-800-799-7233

Helpguide
    Helpguide.org

Women Helping Women
    WomenHelpingWomen.org
    513-391-5610

# The Man Who ...

In the world of Wrong Men, almost every bad dating situation can come to your head as you anticipate that next first date. But sometimes, no mental preparation can get you ready for a right guy and circumstances completely out of anyone's control.

Through any kind of darkness in life, you can find light. Mine was a guy friend who was the light in everyone's life. He accepted everyone he met with a huge smile regardless of who they were and what their situation in life was. Most of my days were spent working with the cops handling my ex-boyfriend, so it was hard to find friends who really understood what I was going through. People had no idea how to act towards me knowing about the situations with my ex, so people often turned away from me or tried to make awkward jokes. However, I had an amazing talent that proved to be very useful in my social life in college, the ability to shotgun large quantities of beer to at least impress people enough to want to have me at the parties. While at one of these parties I met my guy friend.

We were the best of friends and had a lot of fun together from the second we met. He was a wrestler, so my ex tended to suppress his psychopathic tendencies when my guy friend was around. In an effort to take a break from what was going on with my ex, drinking became a main feature in my life, and this is one thing my friend and I had in common. I have story after story of us finding each other at a party only to end up in some field together laughing hysterically or in some other bizarre situation heavily induced by alcohol. At one party we landed in the bathroom together, attempting to wash our pants in the tub. Obviously, it seemed like such an appropriate place to do laundry. Soon enough, the room was pouring suds out into the hallway where everyone was waiting in line for the bathroom. When someone asked us to get out of the bathroom, we decided that this would be great timing for a water fight. No one else seemed to agree with us after the stereo equipment started getting wet and we were soon asked to leave the party completely.

My guy friend and I never had anything physical between us. I refused to get involved with another man after the disaster of my first love. But he remained my friend with no sexual benefits, which I assume is like dangling a steak in front of a dog to a college guy. We'd have sleepovers and he'd crack me up by coming into the room having squeezed into my tiny pants. Every once in a while we'd "sleep skins" where we'd sleep naked in bed together, but still not even sharing a kiss. Yes, I know, this was his attempt at maybe getting to some, but it still wasn't happening.

Every time he would spend the night, I would have this reoccurring dream. In the dream, I was at the bottom of a pool looking up at people who were looking down at me. I knew that I had drowned, but I could see everything that they were doing and how they were talking about me. We would analyze this dream every time with no logical reasoning. Eventually we'd forget about it and our next adventure would come when we'd meet again.

In the back of my head this entire time, I had a grand master plan. I had decided that I was going to wait six months before I got involved with another man to let the situation with my ex cool down, but that the man was going to be my friend when it would happen. It took me years to learn that you may have a plan, but someone else may have a bigger one.

Memorial Day weekend came around and the entire party crew went camping at Lake Shasta. It was pure insanity, bouncing around from campsite to campsite with massive amounts of alcohol from 9 AM until you were passed out in the bushes somewhere. At one point I crawled into my friend's tent with him to snuggle. We joked around because he had cuts all over his face from doing a back flip off of a house boat. He explained to me that he had been drinking and I told him "Someday you're going to kill yourself by drinking." It was one of the few statements in my life I soon wished hadn't been right.

The next day I returned to my guy friend's campsite and he was nowhere to be found. Several people said that he had put on a show of beer-bonging a fifth of vodka and must have jumped on a house boat. The day we were leaving, I returned to see if he made it back OK …

still he was missing. It felt like the second someone told me he hadn't come back was the exact second I heard multiple helicopters flying over my head in a search party. We all had to leave to return to school the next day, but we were one man short. Days later they found his body right below where we were all swimming. After beer-bonging that fifth of vodka, he had gone down to the water to go fishing and never came back.

The entire school showed up for his funeral, and everyone learned something from his passing. Most learned never to allow your friend to beer-bong a fifth of vodka. Others took on the guilt of his passing. Although friends at the time tried to tell me that I had the same drinking habits and to watch out, this wasn't my time to hear that. I took the fear with me for years that if I couldn't reach someone,

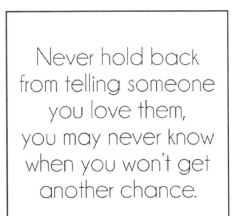

Never hold back from telling someone you love them, you may never know when you won't get another chance.

they might not be alive. However, I took one important lesson. Never hold back from telling someone you love them because you may never know when you won't get another chance.

At the end, the dream made sense. Even though he was under water and we might have conceived him as being gone, he is always around and watching over us.

## Signs You Are Dating A Man Who…:

- This is pretty obvious, don't you think?

## Final Thoughts on a Man Who…

If you've dated someone who has passed away, it will take time, but the pain will subside eventually. This has to happen in your own time frame, and no one knows how much time you will need better than you will. Keep the memories of that person alive and always keep in mind what they brought to your life.

# The Cheater

In any sense of the word, there really isn't anything much worse than dealing with a cheater whether you're dealing with someone snagging money from the Monopoly box, a guy with cards up his sleeve or you catch your significant other in bed with someone else. Cheaters will lie to others, to you, and even to themselves in an attempt to make their conscience fit in with the rule book. Usually, when they cheat in one area of life, they will cheat in others until you're left with the decision of whether or not you'd like to continue playing the game.

Surprisingly with my friend's passing, my first love showed great compassion. One day he walked up to me, gave me a hug and said he was sorry for everything - and I never really saw him again. I look back at his apology now and appreciate the fact that he was aware of the pain he caused and was man enough to own it. Of course, I wasn't sure if this was just the opening scene in "The Crazy Man Returns," so I still was constantly on guard.

While mourning over the death of my friend, I found myself at a house where several of the wrestlers lived in an attempt to feel like I was connecting to him again. In that same time frame, the dog who had become one of the main things that kept me going from day to day got cancer and passed away as well. Somehow, there was one wrestler who, when I was around him, somehow made everything seem to calm down, and the pain of the losses didn't feel as bad. I also didn't fear the harassment from my first love as much anymore so I could actually sleep at night again.

I soon started feeling like one of the guys at the house and the wrestler and I were spending all our time together, drinking beer, floating on rafts at the lake, figuring out how to remove the couch from the roof. You know, the common college stuff. Then there came that one day where our friendship had one too many beers and we started making out. Next thing I knew, we were dating.

There wasn't some magical, sweep me off my feet element to any of this situation. It was as if we just happened to always be in the same group of friends so circumstances made sense for us to date. We quickly became 'the couple' in the big group of friends that everyone just figured, "They're together and that's how it is." No ifs, ands, or buts about it.

Eventually, the days turned into months, which turned into years. Graduation came and went. We walked to grab our diplomas at the same time, threw one last party, then started saying goodbye to people as the crew started going their separate ways. We soon found ourselves in San Diego where my father had moved to.

From time to time, I'd catch my "loving wrestler" flirting with other women with the over-exaggerated excuse that he just had really close friends who were girls and I was 'insecure.'

Things progressively got worse as he once dragged me to one of his girl "friend's" graduation. During the festivities, I found myself sitting on the couch by myself for most of the night in a room full of strangers wondering where the only person I knew, my boyfriend, had gone. Minutes went by, then well over an hour passed. Finally, I made my way up to her bedroom to see where he had been spending his time with this "friend" of his who was sitting there whining to him about something on her bed. Gee... could it be that he was dating someone? No, probably just a bad hair day. I questioned the situation to get his almost pre-recorded response on the matter that, "She's only a Friend!" and "You're crazy!" This was when I realized that if a man is doing something wrong, he will play the "crazy" card on you.

Through the downfalls of this relationship, there was one aspect that falsely assured me that I was with right person. The two men who I had consistently sought for affection from had finally found each other, the wrestler and my father. I'm pretty sure this part of my relationship would be the only time you'd hear "So Happy Together" as the theme song. I think my dad saw a lot of himself in him. He was a wrestler growing up and shot off into a successful career in engineering through government contracts in the emerging computer industry, NASA, electronics, and finally ended up working at one of the major tech companies until he retired. The wrestler finally started to respect someone in the relationship, but unfortunately it wasn't me. I applied everywhere around our new town looking for work and going through the tedious interview process. The wrestler's application slid to the top of the hiring pile at the company where my father worked and he was quickly escorted into a very plush job with an insane beginning salary for a recent college grad including complete benefits and a 401K.

A few weeks later he was fired, leaving me to be the lone bread winner, and gave him more time to develop his skills at playing Nintendo. I resented his complete lack of attempting to get a job, but I absolutely loved being a graphic designer in the working world. Ever since I was a little girl I dreamed of a day when I would have my own successful business, a loving husband, and a great family of my own. I know, not your standard little girl's dreams, but I'm not your standard little girl. So this was one step in the right direction. After eight months of being a professional video game player, with a side job of looking at questionable websites, the wrestler got his job back again with little to no effort on his part. He and my father were happy again.

At the time, I was reading investment books, and I decided that buying a house would be a lot better use of my money than making someone else rich on our rental home. Soon, we were on our way to joint home ownership. I didn't know it at the time, but this "investment" would become another expensive albatross to our ever-failing relationship.

Four years passed by, and even though the wrestler chipped away even more at my self-esteem by scrutinizing my every move and constantly throwing his attachments to other women in my face, I enjoyed the peace of not having dramatic scenes or people dying on me. I couldn't help but feel desperate for a slight fragment of affection or consideration from him, while still knowing that we had nothing in common. However, I always had that drink that gave me the much needed attention. Drinking remained in the scene as I coped with a bottle of wine a night to avoid the fact that I was miserable. I spent many nights sitting and crying, feeling so lonely because he was extremely busy with the fifteenth football game that he had tuned into for the night.

Even though my relationship was a disaster, I found my one new love in life was business. At home, there were neglect and insults, where out in the business world I found accolades and appreciation. I went into a sales position and had an award-winning career during this time. It wasn't the business I had dreamt of owning my entire life, but I was stimulated, aggressive, and ready to make things happen.

Years into the relationship, I realized that it wasn't moving anywhere. In my head, I planned on ending it after we came back from a trip I had won to London. This is where things should have ended, but, from what I can only assume came from the wrestler's desire to make my father happy he decided to take things one step further.

One day, while we were looking at cannons at Edinburgh Castle he attempted a speech from *Braveheart* and asked me to marry him. He didn't have a ring, so I will never know if he had planned to pop the question or if it was a last minute decision, but out of my desire to feel wanted, I said "Yes." At this point, I fell for one of the biggest assumptions people make in a relationship. The assumption where you think once that ring slides on your finger, your fairy godmother waves her magic wand over your relationship magically whisking away any trouble or bad personality traits in the other person as you ride off into the sunset to your happily ever after. I was soon to find out that the reason the relationship hadn't already moved anywhere was because it had nowhere else to go. And a "Happily Ever After" in this situation was going to be more of the same ol despair.

Through the next year, I distracted myself from the complete dysfunction of my relationship and planned a wedding. Family members around at the time expressed frequently to me what a wonderful husband he would be and how well he treated me, completely oblivious to the reality. At every decision, the wrestler would bail out of what I asked him to do to move the wedding forward, and my workaholic tendencies would just pick up the pieces because, well, when I say I'm going to do something, I do it!

The day of my wedding came, one of the worst days of my life. I had the most beautiful layout, bridesmaids, and dress at a stunning winery in the hills. Every aspect of the day was planned to perfection with the décor, officiants, and music. When my father took my arm to walk me down the isle, he looked at me and said, "This is going to be a wonderful marriage." We got through the insanely long service, and, as we were ready for pictures, my beautiful day turned black. My maid of honor leaned over me and said, "Who is that trashy girl?" I had no idea, so I asked my new husband. Turns out, he had taken some time from his last trip back to his home town to see his ex-girlfriend and invite her to the wedding. She had come from one state to another in order to attend a wedding where she wasn't invited. My husband soon declared that it was more important that she be there than me. In somewhat of a daze, I finished out the rest of the day, confused about what was going on. I guess my feelings weren't hidden well enough, since even his mom told him that it looked as though I had lost my soul.

Of course, I got drunk. After getting on the plane to Jamaica for our honeymoon, I drank more and landed in a place that offered all inclusive drinks! This was a prime setup for someone who had to play "side interest" to another woman on her own wedding day. In the spirit of my Rastafarian surroundings, I thought Bob Marley was right about my wedding disaster and 'No Woman' really would have meant 'No Cry' when it came to some ex-girlfriend showing up at my wedding. The thing was, he didn't seem to care. There were no apologies or concern of how I had felt. He believed that inviting an ex-girlfriend I didn't even know to a wedding my father paid a fortune for was appropriate. In the back of my mind, I hoped that this was just some last hurrah between the two and she would be gone for good, but, once we got home, then she just started calling the house.

Several months passed as I was in denial. To keep pain at bay, I threw myself into on starting my own business. I worked hard and made a decent amount of money in those few months. One day I was meeting at a restaurant with my accountant, my husband randomly walked in. I was so excited to show him how well I had been doing. In what I could only interpret as jealousy of my success, he left the restaurant irritated, and began to dig the further descent of being one of the worst relationships of my life. Hindering the excitement of my long-term success, I have yet to ever earn as much as I had in those first few months.

The one thing he was providing me, help with the finances, was in jeopardy, and when he felt I was exceeding him on that, he no longer cared to even try in the relationship. Soon he found another girl "friend" at work and lost all hints of showing respect to me or his co-workers, some of whom were at my wedding and all of whom greatly respected my father. Of course, he kept up with his "friend" strategy so I decided to play along.

All of a sudden, my husband developed an interest in yoga. One would think, being his wife and all, I'd be invited along, but this was not the case. It was very clear something was going on here. Although I questioned it, it wasn't a sudden interest in men's spandex yoga pants. I decided at the last minute one day to join him without giving him the opportunity of warning his little lady before coming to class. 24 Hour Fitness, as always, attempted to put their high pressure sales force on me before joining the class. That day, I found out that the easiest way to get out of one of their sales pitches is just to say, "This is what I want to do; I won't join your gym, but I'd like to go to this one yoga class because my husband is screwing around with some girl in there." Speechless, the salesman gave me a day pass. When his new little fling walked in, her jaw dropped as I waved at her with a big shit-eating grin. Surprisingly, she stayed through the whole class but quickly ran out the door with her mat the second it ended. That's so weird. I thought they were friends. I didn't even get a hello!

From time to time, I'd get a phone call when he was out with friends and hear her voice in the background. It was when his work had a talk with him about the fact that he and this girl where flown up to San Francisco for a meeting together but never showed up that my father got pissed. My husband could no longer look my dad in the eyes. At that point my father told me, "That Company will not get involved unless something completely inappropriate is going on. You need to get out of this." But I still wanted it to get fixed, "It" being my marriage. I took a vow and it was completely out of my comprehension how someone could also share such a vow and have it mean nothing.

I tried every angle possible to try to save my failing marriage. My feelings cycled through confusion, to assumptions that I must have done something wrong, to anger, to desperate pleas for him to help me create a loving relationship. The confusion was met with answers when he admitted that every instance in our past that I felt instinctually uncomfortable in relationship to another woman was because there really was something going on either physically or emotionally. My 'wrong doings' seemed miniscule when he proclaimed his frustrations with me stemmed from the fact that I wouldn't fill up the ice cube trays and interrupted football games. The desperate pleas were contradicted when I was actively buying books on saving my marriage only to spot a book on the coffee table about "How to get a divorce." And my anger was only subsided by the hope that snuck through the words of a counselor when he said "You need to find someone who loves you."

The day came that he had someone serve me with divorce papers. It was the day I learned that it takes two people to get married and one person to get a divorce. I told him at the time that if I sign them, that's it. I'd never talk to him again except for carrying out the guidelines of the split. He responded saying, "Someday we'll look back and laugh at this." Over a decade later, I find little about this situation funny other than the approach I took to it. I held true to my word, packed up my stuff, and moved back up to Oregon. He stayed in the house that my father helped us buy, with the job my father helped him get. I got shafted out of my home, out of my life, and had to restart fulfilling my dreams, but I know I got the best part of the deal when I drove away with the puppy I loved so much.

Months later, a mutual friend of mine called me. She nervously explained how my husband had asked her and her husband through the years to go on trips with him and the girl who showed up at my wedding. The validation from other people was always nice, but the pain of betrayal was very hard to overcome. Just as I thought he would, my ex-husband started reaching out in delusional e-mails and phone calls wanting to talk, but I completely ignored him. My father received a rambling e-mail from him in an attempt to justify his behavior with the girl at work because his wife (me) was so terrible. I guess an ice-chilled drink is really that important to some people.

Before my ex-husband got together with me, he didn't date much except for a girl in high school. It left me with the knowledge that men need to get out before committing. After this disaster, I would never date another man who hadn't gotten the running around out of his system. By no means do I think men should behave like man whores, but they should at least have the decency to get it out of their system without a false commitment to anyone.

I learned that just because the insanity of your life settles down when you're with someone, you don't need to settle down with them. You shouldn't settle until you're with someone who lets you be yourself. Don't conform to what the "Wrong Man" or a family member tells you is right or even what society claims is worthy. The wrong men won't be around long. Your family might not know much about you other than your genetic makeup. A society that glamorizes reality stars who use the corner of a bar as their bathroom should not be one you conform to or aim to impress. In the end, bitterness fades, pain will disappear, but you should never respect someone who gives you no reason to.

I started realizing the similarities of my relationship with my ex-husband to my parents' relationship. They dated in college, got married and whisked each other away into several bleak decades. Had I subconsciously taken their recipe for dysfunction and followed the same path? Some girls unknowingly spend their whole life searching for a relationship like their parent's. I'm just glad I got mine out of the way early.

There will be some relationships in your life that you can't find the good in them. For me, this was one of them. In all reality, the ending of this marriage opened doors for a bright future that I didn't know existed. During this split a phrase that a friend of mine said to me consistently resonated in my head. "The best thing my ex ever did for me was divorce me."

## Signs You Are Dating a Cheater:

- They disappear – Blocks of time will be missing from their day that they have no excuse for.

- Selfish – Cheaters care about one person, themselves. This is apparent in anything they do.

- Sudden changes in behavior (yoga classes?), clothes (spandex?), etc., and he will not elaborate why these changes are being made.

- They get defensive when caught in lies. Think about it, if you were at the store for an hour, would you feel the need to scream that fact at your partner? No, you'd just go grab the receipt and show it to her with the date and time. Trusting relationships have no problem showing the receipts.

- He's done it before – I've heard several stories from people in high school who had cheated and learned quickly why you don't cheat, but adolescence is the last time the "Once a Cheater, Always A Cheater" gets excused. If you know that your significant other has a history of cheating, he is a self-serving person and he may never figure out how hurtful his behavior is.

- The phones say it all! Trusting relationships have no problem using each other's phones. Think back to the days when there was just one line at the house. You never saw someone locking up the line so his spouse couldn't get on it, did you? If you're not doing anything wrong, your significant other should be able to use your phone if she feels like it because there's nothing to hide. However, if he's the type to delete his messages and call log, there's always the ability to examine the activity on the phone bill.

- Depending on their job, if they're always "Working Late."

- The classic lipstick on the collar.

- They accidentally call you another girl's name.

- Another woman's clothing at his place when he has no sister.

## Final Thoughts on Dating a Cheater

It drives me crazy when people say, "Oh, she has to know he's cheating on her," because you don't. Cheaters will try to twist things around on you to convince you that you are just making things up in your head. You may hear it straight from the cheaters that you're being cheated on, you may catch them in the act, you may not find out for decades after the fact, or you may never know the truth. What I do know now is that it's better to leave a situation that you are constantly questioning what is going on than to stay in it. Whether you want to take the time and emotional effort to play private investigator or keep wondering how to get the truth of a situation with a cheater, your heart knows the truth of whether or not a person can make you happy, so listen to it.

# A Girl and Her Dog

A moment needs to be taken out of my wrong man story to feature the one male who, tried and true, never let me down and was always by my side. This was Kavic, my beautiful Alaskan Malamute dog who survived through the divorce with me as we set out on our adventures in life together.

Going through a divorce will show you who your friends are. The people solely in your life for the good times disappear when things start going bad. You'll also have friends who try and try to be by your side, but have no comprehension as to what you're going through, and they'll just fade away while watching you go through the mourning of your lost life. I've had friends who were only my friends when I was single. Then I had friends who were only my friends when I was in a relationship. But through all the good and bad, I always had one little guy who was my reason to wake up in the morning. When people would greet me with false pity or avoid me with confusion, Kavic would come running up to me day after day with the biggest smile on his face ready to take on the world. How could I let him down!

He kept me going. Every day, I knew that we had to go on several walks or he would throw a dramatic scene. In contrast to my first love, somehow he was able to get away with it because he was so damn cute. I had to keep active so he could get his exercise. I had to keep meeting new people because he would find a way to socialize with every person, plant or animal, within a mile radius. And I had to keep working so I could afford the things that to kept him happy. Of course, it's questionable if it was necessary for me to buy a new car or move into a new house purely because I knew they'd be better for him, but I have no regrets.

Kavic was heaven sent. Everyone going through a hard time needs something to keep them up and everyone going through great times needs a Kavic to celebrate with.

## Signs You Are Dating a Dog:

- If you relate to many of the stories in this book, although you are not dating an animal in the canine species, you could most likely be dating a dog.

- They are fluffy and go the bathroom outside… most of the time.

## Final Thoughts on Pets and Your Single Life

The best pet owners know that their pet is their child. When you're single, they're your confidant and best friend. But while in a relationship, the interactions between your pets and the person you're dating can add a dimension into whether or not you're dating the right person. Of course, there are the occasional overly-dependent pets that will not let any other living, breathing thing come into contact with you, but generally speaking.

The most extreme case I know of was my best friend from college and Maid of Honor. She was engaged to a guy who insisted she move in with him. She hesitated moving to the middle of nowhere but thought that since they were getting married, it was time to make the move. She packed up all her belongings and her two kitties ready for the move. When they were moved in, her fiancé surprisingly told her that her cats were not welcome and they had to live outside. Her cats were spoiled like nothing you'd ever seen before with a plush life of extra food, consistent brushing, and only a mere peak into the outdoors when they would go on the back patio to watch birds. My friend, with great hesitation, agreed to the 'outdoor cat' plan. Within a few weeks, both cats had died from things that came with living in an outdoor environment. My friend eventually called off the wedding and added, "Wrong Man Who Killed My Cats" to her dating memoirs.

Through the years, my dog had every range of emotional interaction with men I knew. Some he loved and sprinted to greet at the door. He growled at others, destroyed their belongings, or went into massive depression when they were gone.

# The Red Piece of Paper

Obviously, things weren't working out for me in my love life. I had people telling me from every angle what to do in relationships, how and when to recover from a bad one, what made me happy, what I should do, what I should read, what I should be. I was exhausted! I got to the point where I was in a battle with what people wanted from me and who I really was. I had attempted a marriage without even knowing what works for me. I remember taking a "relationship" quiz in a magazine and realized absolutely none of the qualities of my previous partners made me happy. Whether I inherited the behavior, or developed them myself, I was in a cycle of dating people who I did not mesh well with. The cycle needed to be broken. So, I set on a mission to define exactly what I needed in my perfect partner, then break the pattern that had been instilled in my head of what a relationship should be.

What did I need? Not my family, not random people so sure of what I was looking for. Me. I'm pretty sure I read every best-selling relationship book at the time and analyzed what I needed in the future to be happy. If I stated that I wanted "Respect," I'd tear it down so I knew what respect looked like in a relationship - the interactions, the actions a person does with another to show respect, everything. Of

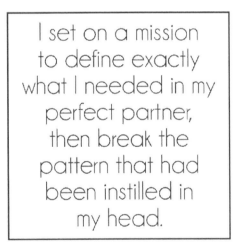

I set on a mission to define exactly what I needed in my perfect partner, then break the pattern that had been instilled in my head.

course, with me, a big hitter was NOT to bring other women to intimate personal events.

I was so cheesy as to write out all the qualities I thought I needed in a man on a red piece of paper. The words on this paper were the epitome of my perfect match. He'd treat me with love and respect, we'd dance together, his smile would light up any room, and when we were together, it was like we were taking on the world as our own little team. Descriptive words covered an entire sheet. That paper stayed with me through the years, tucked away in my top drawer as a reference to what I was looking for so I could match it up to any prospects. Referring to this paper allowed me to call myself out when I started dating the "Wrong Man" that filled the remaining chapters of this book!

# The Rebound

When a rival in basketball misses a shot, a rebound is an opportunity to turn things around and put the game in your favor. However, when the term is applied to relationships, rebounds are synonymous with gasps, and "oh no, you don't want to do that" conversations with your friends. Coming out of a relationship, we assume and wish our rebound will bounce back like a basketball and give us a chance to win again. Perhaps you're the next Lebron James, and this approach will work out for you, or you might find yourself another Wrong Man to throw into the basket.

Divorce, for me, was a nightmare. I couldn't tell if I missed the companionship of a partner who had never really been there, disturbed by the fact that there were human beings with absolutely no comprehension of how they hurt other people, or realized that I married one! My body went into the drastic cycle of a breakup where I would lose a ton of weight by not eating, to splurging on ice cream, to staying up all night watching infomercials hallucinating that George Foreman was my new best friend. To top it off, everyone around me tagged me with a "damaged" stigma due to the divorce. Little did they know I was damaged way before that, but now people had a label they could put on me. I guess I started noticing I was getting pathetic. There were days I'd sit on my friend's couch drinking wine, crying, and developing a deeply intellectual dialog between her several cats. As entertaining as it apparently was to her teenage daughters, I was turning into the cat lady, fast. Many people had said, "You should move on" mainly to encourage me to move past how my ex-husband had "moved on" to other women even when contracted to marriage. But I decided it was time to get back out there and see what other options there were.

There are so many sayings that we live by these days. Most of them we find popping up on our social media accounts with some kind of graphic and a "Like" button. But one phrase that will come up constantly as a single person is that "People will come into your life for a reason, a season or a lifetime." This next Wrong Man came into my life for a reason, stayed maybe a season, and only in this book will he stay for a lifetime.

My husband just divorced me after years of criticizing my personality and throwing other women in my face, so having a guy who admired me was a fascinating surprise. My "Reason Guy" did exactly this. In high school, we had dated for a little while before my first love, and Reason Guy said that he had feelings for me from back then.

It was pretty cute. It was as though he felt he was first in line on a waiting list and he didn't wait long to ask me out, to make sure he didn't miss out this time around. For me, it was great to feel wanted after the crap stack that had just been flung at my face. We started doing things that we might have done when we were young together. We played soccer and went on trips to the beach. This seemed exciting and innocent, like the days back in high school, but we'd soon find out that neither of us were the people we were in our teens. He had briskly jumped through his years of high school, prom, and frat parties, and then he waltzed into the working world with little in his way. My counter-life of abusive relationships, deaths, and signing divorce papers was completely foreign to him. Having only been in his mid-twenties, he had not experienced the painful things I had been through and didn't relate to some of my hurtful past. A lot of people in their twenties have never seen the negative side of life, and some never will. He was one of them at the time.

For eight months, we dated despite the fact that I was completely dysfunctional. He was a mask for the underlying issues I had from the whirlwind of my first three wrong men stories, but he was necessary at that time in my life. Another saying that people live by is that "moving, changing jobs, and going through a divorce are three of the most difficult events in your life," and I was taking on all three at the same time. When I moved up to Oregon, I decided I was going to try to take my business with me, maintaining some clients from California and seeking to find more locally. While the "moving" and "changing jobs" aspect of my life were in massive flux, Reason Guy put a hold on dealing with my relationship issues while I took care of getting other important aspects set up for my new life.

But the day came when we just didn't make sense anymore. We were not in high school and I was too broken for a relationship to go on in a meaningful way with someone who had lived a happy-go-lucky life. So we went our separate ways.

During this breakup, my friend's mother said to me, "You're always in relationships. You need to just take a break from it all." I always found this ironic coming from a woman who stayed with a husband who had one of the most treacherous affairs I've ever seen, but I took her advice and gave my love life some space.

I found at this time that I was going to have to deal with things in one way or the other. I had mastered the art of faking happiness as a child, but my body wasn't going to let me get away with it any more. I developed insomnia. I'm convinced that my doctor at the time caved to every prescription drug rep who came through her door and turned every office visit into her own little personal infomercial. I was prescribed a new "addiction free" sleep aid until she realized I was addicted to it only to move on to the next brand. I'm pretty sure she ran out of free sleep aid samples when her diagnosis changed and she gave me some anti-depressants.

About one to a month later, I knew that was no solution for me. Yes, I was depressed and upset and I couldn't sleep, but living life feeling anything, even bad things, was better than the numb trance that junk put me in. I went back to her office one day and said, "Listen, I'm not taking those pills anymore. I feel like shit because someone massively screwed me over! I have every right to feel this way. I refuse to cater to a society that tries to make victims feel shameful about the fact that they are in pain. What we really need to do is start focusing on distributing drugs to give to these selfish jerks who live their lives screwing everyone else over."

I was far from cured of insomnia, but I chose my drug free path and I was on my way. I started going to counseling to deal with some issues and began to find traces of the person I was so long ago before any man started strong-arming me into being something I wasn't.

## Signs You Are Dating a Rebound:

- You haven't moved past the fact that your ex was a blithering idiot.

- You are analyzing everything you do in the relationship because your ex has told you that that everything you do is horrible.

- You can't stop questioning your new guy about why your ex would treat you so badly.

## Final Thoughts on Dating a Rebound

When you have been completely cheated on and are out of a marriage or any horrific relationship, you think it's only fair that you should find someone right away who will be the knight in shining armor to that horrific experience. Odds are, it's not going to happen right away. The best things to do is to learn how to get past what happened and figure out how to make yourself happy again.

# Finding Guidance in Life

When sorting out the troubles of my past, I looked at things in life that would guide me to happiness. I came up with this theory that, based on the pure rules of Karma, if I lead my life to be a good person in every way, I won't be in another situation like the ones I had in the past. Then, walking into a Rotary Club one day, I found a simple outline that I would try to use from that day forward in all of my life decisions.

Rotary is a nonprofit organization that has clubs all around the world. People in the clubs donate their time and money to put together community service projects that benefit humanitarian concerns in their direct community and internationally.

The club I walked into was one that recited the code that would change my life:

*The Rotary Four Way Test: In all the thing we say think or do:*

1) *Is it the Truth?*
2) *Is it Fair to All Concerned?*
3) *Will it Bring Good Will and Better Friendship?*
4) *Will it Be Beneficial to All Concerned?*

This wrapped everything up for me. I set out to not only squash any little white lie that attempted to come out of my mouth, but it was really the first time I realized that I was part of this "All" they talked about. This was about creating fair and beneficial environments for everyone involved, including myself. Before this point in my life, I had been so concerned about making any man I was in a relationship with happy, I never thought about the fact that a situation will only be prosperous if everyone in it is benefitting.

I was in Rotary for a total of 6 years with perfect attendance and was President for a term. I helped with projects locally and all around the world, ended up building their marketing materials and websites, and became a leader in the district.

I was so pro-Rotary that, on one occasion, I would use the principles to ward off "Wrong Men" who spoke at a Rotary event. At a leadership training event for young adults that I attended, a psychologist was speaking to about 100 people in their twenties. Although a lot of what he said was decent material, he started trying to mislead the group into encouraging secrecy of infidelity in marriage. He threw out a "hypothetical situation" about a man who went to Chicago on work and had an affair. He started to say that if you were in a situation like that, you need to keep your infidelity to yourself because telling your significant other would just be a burden on them. What a bunch of crap! Everyone in the room could tell this wasn't a hypothetical story. This was him trying to make excuses for something he did. I raised my hand and just started talking without being called on. "I'm sorry, this does not fit in with the Four Way Test. Look up at the banner on the wall behind you. Number one, 'Is it the truth?' This is the Rotary guidelines. Are you telling us to go against it? I've been in a relationship where the husband is running around behind my back and I sure as hell would have wanted to hear the truth a lot sooner so I could get out of that miserable situation." Looking around the room, shock was on everyone's face. Strangely, the guy excused himself, needing a break. Everyone started laughing and asking things like "Yea, buddy, how was Chicago?"

If you want anything to change in your life, you need to make some changes. Rotary and the Four Way Test gave me the tools to start making them.

# Men with Terrible Timing

Someone once told me that three things need to be in line when you start dating someone: attraction, beliefs, and timing. There is a tendency for us to make exception after exception to try to mold whoever we find into the person of our dreams. Of the three, nothing is more irritating than the uncontrollable dating factor of bad timing.

There was a reunion for my high school where every class that had ever graduated was invited. I wasn't that interested in hanging out with the judgmental trust fund babies who thought the kind of insanity that I had been through with my exes was just something you'd see on the Lifetime channel, but somehow the few friends I had in that scene convinced me to go. And, hey, there was an open bar. Little did I know, one of the few people from my high school who would be in my life a lot longer than anyone else was someone I hadn't even met back in my school days, but someone I'd meet at that party.

All the girls who had been in my class were gawking over two guys who had been freshmen when we were seniors. Growing up had done them well! I believe the term "Beef Hunk" was used. One of them had joined the Army. We chatted a little in a group conversation. Then, after a few drinks and several jokes towards people's snide remarks of my divorce, I walked up to this Army Boy, throwing him my car keys. "Hey, are you sober? Drive my car." The guy lied, shaking his head yes, and we were on our way to the next bar stop for the party train.

We sat parked on the side of the road where he proceeded to tell me all about myself with great fascination. Apparently, I was the hot girl in high school, and I had no idea! He told me how he and his friends would talk about me growing up. His personal feelings seemed disproportionate to me when he compared me to a super model. I was blown away! Apparently, he didn't see all the horrible things my exes had seen in me. Of course, I hadn't had the opportunity to interrupt a football game that night, but I was open arms with this delusion he had created.

Never in my life had I heard such amazing things about another person, let alone myself! With all the wonderful thoughts he had about me from back in school, he never had the nerves to act on them years ago. Maybe it was his new-found confidence in joining the military, but that night he didn't let much get in the way of stealing his first kiss. We drove down the street and made out in a parking lot, but didn't let things go too far. Although I somehow butt dialed one of my friends who ended up hearing the whole thing and insisted more was going on.

Just as horribly timed as his entrance into my life, his exit came a few days later when he left for his duty station. But this would not be his last chapter in my life. We kept in contact through the years. He had impeccable timing of calling me when I was at my lowest, and he was always ready to boost my ego. The phrase "Good ol' Army Boy" became well-known between my friends and me. True to his profession, he was always there behind me, strongly holding me up on some pedestal that no one else could see. So from that point on, no matter what was happening in the political arena, I always supported the troops to return the favor.

When you read this story, hopefully you will see that just because you see a pretty face, it doesn't mean that anyone else in the world has ever told them they were beautiful. Even if they're in their late 20's, it also doesn't mean they automatically feel worthy of love or desirable. If you are that person who thinks you don't have that beauty, inside or out, know that everyone is beautiful and desirable in one way or in many ways. You might just be surrounding yourself with people who either can't see it or refuse to tell you.

## Signs You're Dating a Man With Bad Timing:

- UHaul, boxes, or a plane ticket.

- You met him on a vacation.

- One or the other of you is always single when the other is not.

- He just broke up with your best friend.

## Final Thoughts on Dating a Man With Bad Timing

I've had friends who have gotten completely infatuated with men they found at the wrong time in their lives. I've seen girls hold out for, obsess about, and, Yes, online stalking guys that were only available to them for an hour or two. If the person has it, they have it and no time or distance can stop what the future may hold. You might find love, you might find a friend, or you might find more trouble down the road.

# Men Who Are Too Young

For the second time in your life, after that kindergarten trip to the zoo, there will come a day where you find that cougars have made a major come back. This is usually in your late twenties. It doesn't take Demi Moore to tell you that sometimes you'll find a spark with a much younger man than some of the worn down emotionally-jaded older men. In fact, being a cougar has become so hot that usually all it takes is walking into your local bar to have a swarm of younger men approach you to buy you a drink or play a round of 'Let me guess your age' when you hint at the fact that they're too young. The gamble comes when you decide take the chance to see if the number of his years can balance out with the quality of your relationship.

The series Sex and The City is every broken-hearted person's best friend. Many times in my single life, I've watched from season one to six back to back, almost as part of my break up strategy. Nothing will get you through breakups better than that TV series, good friends, and a bottle of wine. I think most people can identify with one, if not all four of the main characters. Some of my friends prided themselves on being the Carrie, talented but always flustering through her selection of wrong men. Others were Miranda, the hard working, straight-forward redhead. As if lying to themselves, many claimed themselves to be the innocent and ever-positive Charlotte. In my changes of strategies while I attempted each of the characters on the show in my relationships, at this time in my life, I was interested in Samantha's approach of never really getting too attached to men and just having physical relationships with them. I thought, "What a great idea! I'll never get hurt again!" On this mission, I too soon found out why Samantha's character is not found much in the real world, but how tempting someone like her boy toy Smith Jarrod can be.

On Mission Samantha, I would go out with my friends not looking for men, but having a great time dancing and finding our ladies' nights around town. There was one bar called Wichita's where ladies' drinks were 50 cents on Thursdays, so you know where you'd find us. One particular Thursday, a friend of mine spotted a guy and said, "He's cute! Go hit on him!" Picking up on a guy, to me, always felt similar to the way you feel when you're on a diving board not knowing if the water is going to be cold or not. I'd always stand there, mentally preparing myself, then take the jump. I had been joking around for months about bad pickup lines, and I didn't care at all what would happen with this guy, so I just decided to use one. "Hi, I work in the lubrication industry and we're looking to hire". "Where do I apply?" he said with a heart-melting smile. Thus, began my relationship with The Youngeon.

He was 22 years old at the time and when he looked at me, I had a familiar feeling. I had gotten this feeling when I was little for my first love, but my perception of love and relationships was so distorted I had no idea what I was feeling. He was sexy. I wanted to ask him if he had just walked off of an Abercrombie and Fitch bag. This was back in the day when those models actually had muscles and didn't look like twelve-year-old boys. Throughout the night we couldn't stop staring into each other's eyes and more than once I said, "Do I know you?" I felt as if I had known him my entire life.

On our first date, I was still on Mission Samantha and determined not to care about another man. After talking for awhile, he stated that he had been hurt in the past and didn't want to get attached to someone again. Hmm, this sounded familiar. He then said how he'd love something physical without the attachment. Hmm... that sounded "Samantha" to me and what better guy to hang out with than one so attractive!

Things soon led to our physical romance, but I don't think either of us knew how to just keep things physical. We'd stay up all night messing around, talking, then messing around again. We'd have the deepest discussions and wouldn't leave each other for days. When we went places together, it was as if we were the only ones in the room. As attractive as he was, he never looked at another girl in my presence, and I felt wonderful because of it. For the first time ever in my dating history, I felt I could be myself. I had been constantly belittled by men to the point where I was insecure about everything, even down to my sense of humor. Somehow the Youngeon allowed me to be myself and when I was free to be myself, we had the most fun together.

Our commonalities didn't stop, and I soon found out he had a mischievous side that matched my own. On one day, we were driving back from a movie out in farm country when we saw a massive amount of cars at an alpaca farm. "Let's crash that party," I said somewhat joking. Then he pulled into the driveway. When we got there, we saw a few teenagers go inside. "Holy! We're at a high school party!" We laughed in the car and started talking again. As always, our talking led to other things and next thing we knew, there was one steamed up Trooper at this kid party. We didn't think anyone was around so the Youngeon took things to another level as he got out of the car completely naked. He started peeing in the bushes as cars drove by and he waved. After jumping back in the car and putting all our clothes back on, there was a tap on the window, and we were asked to leave.

From time to time, his age would show through. The topic of 'What were you like in high school?' came up all too often for a woman in her late 20's. All I could tell him was that a lot of time had passed and I wasn't really sure. Of course, any reference to a pop culture or song reference from the 80's was wasted and left him staring at me blankly in a world of confusion. But for the most part, his maturity level matched mine and we had a great time.

Things with the Youngeon and me heated up on every level, and I started to realize what that feeling was that I had from the first second I met him. It was that "Meant to Be" feeling, and I was falling in love with him. I had been looking for that person who I could be myself with and just have fun with, and he was right there.

> The bubbly of my drinks rarely added a bubbly quality to my relationships.

Then came the catch. When the Youngeon was around, things felt so amazing, but when he was gone, I never knew if he'd ever come back. No texts, no phone calls. I had no idea if he was with someone else, lost in a Costco somewhere, or my worst fear - that he had died.

My birthday came and even though we had made plans days in advance, I hadn't heard from him and wasn't sure what was going on. I freaked out thinking that he discovered the worst of me, like my inability to fill an ice cube tray and that he was abandoning me. Resorting to old bad habits, I started drinking… A lot. I got so hammered that I passed out in my bed. I had no idea that he had come to my house later that night ringing the doorbell and calling my phone. I was dead to the world. After realizing I had done this, I started reconsidering my relationship with alcohol. I had to realize that the bubbly of my drinks rarely added a bubbly quality to my relationships. In short, getting sloshed to the point that I had no idea what happened the night before no longer seemed like a feature I wanted to bring to a relationship.

Valentine's Day was a week later, and we were back on for the night. This time, I had valid confirmation that we were getting together. I opened the door to him holding a single red rose. We made dinner together, watched a movie, and went upstairs. When I was in the bathroom, I heard a bunch of shuffling and came out to find him with a four-foot big red bow on his chest. It was one of the cutest things I had ever seen. I was absolutely in love with him, and that was exactly what neither of us set out for.

The next day we talked, and I told him how I was feeling. He confirmed that he was still at the point where he did not want anything serious. I didn't want to get in too deep, so our days were running short. Finally the day came when I called him and said I couldn't spend time with him anymore with these feelings, knowing they weren't reciprocated. That call was so hard to make, but then he said something that changed my approach. "I just kind of figure you're like my exercise bike. You're what I'll use until the real thing comes around." Completely shocked that someone would say this out loud, I realized just how young he was and stated, "I'm not your exercise bike. Thank you for your time." Then we were done, for the time being.

At some point in your life, you may convince yourself that you can have a purely physical relationship. However, I have yet to see this successfully work where neither person in the party falls for the other. I decided it was best to keep things real. Either a relationship had to have the physical, intellectual, spiritual, and friendship qualities, or I wasn't going to have any of it.

Youngeon raised my standard. After having someone I connected so well with on every level, I didn't want anything else. I never would go back to being in a relationship where someone wouldn't let me be who I really was. I felt so connected to him, yet I understood that he had to go out into the world and experience life more. I thought my feelings for him would fade soon, but I was wrong. As far as my Sex and the City character similarities, I found that I exemplified traits of all the show's fabulous girls in the end, plus the unique ones of my own.

## Signs You Are Dating a Man Who's Too Young

- He's always asking about a time period, like high school, that seems lifetimes ago.

- He has no understanding of any pop culture reference from your childhood.

- Judging by his outfit, you're not sure if you're supposed to drop him off at work or at the closest high school.

- You're driving him everywhere because he lost his skateboard.

- He has yet to call you, but is able to frequently text… LOL.

- You catch yourself saying "When I was your age…"

- He uses some new slang that you have no idea what he is talking about.

- He has that amazing body… but isn't sure what to do with it.


## Final Thoughts on Dating a Man Who's Too Young

Age truly is a number. And, at one point age becomes irrelevant. But maturity, on the other hand, is something a little harder to gauge with a calendar. You can have a wonderful, loving relationship that doesn't have the connection of the time period of your younger years because soon the years in your relationship will become more me important. The challenge lies in seeing if your younger man's maturity matches up to their approach in your relationship.

# Faith and Insomnia

I don't know if it is abandonment, the feelings of being deceived or loneliness, but a majority of my friends and I would enter a life of incredible insomnia after our break ups or divorces. And it completely sucked! These are the times in your life you just want to sleep away a few months hoping to wake up with all the pain subsided. Instead, you are left doing the frustrating dance of lay on right side, lay on left side, stare at ceiling, fridge, TV, repeat until that first crack of morning sun that starts peeping up as if to say "You lose!" The best thing insomnia can do is give you time to think and time to discover what changes might need to be done in your life that will leave you, hopefully, sleeping sound.

Ironically at this time in my life, the song "Faith" by George Michael was on my phone, yet I had been fighting the actual meaning of it my whole life. My parents dragged our family off to church every Sunday when we were young. That seemed like complete punishment when MTV was a brand new station and we had videos we needed to watch.

As a child, most of my memories of church were jokes between my father and the pastor who was one of his best friends, eating Cheerios, and sneaking communion wine with my little friends. However, one word from one sermon stuck in my head through my lifetime. Hope. And through all the years of forcing me to go to church, it was the one message God knew I needed to take with me through the years of dating the "Wrong Men."

Going to church while in high school, there were times I was singled out and scrutinized because of my belief in evolution. My father being a scientist always threw a different aspect into my life that churches rarely understood. I also went to a private school where I met most of the living famous scientists in a science and lecture series. The youth pastor at my church once pulled me aside to tell me that he hated having me around because I was too smart and open-minded, and I screwed up his demonstrations. On another occasion, I was kicked out of a mission trip because I went to a Guns and Roses concert. I didn't just feel like I was giving up on God, I felt like he was pushing me out! I knew a lot of the stories from the Bible but never felt connected to God. Through the heartaches and pain from loss, I was convinced that God had no part in my life. I remember writing a paper in college about how He didn't exist. My writing teacher scowled at that.

Through those years, faith had lost me, and I had lost it. Now, a few years after my divorce, the brokenness in my heart was still there. I wanted out of how I felt, and I was looking everywhere for answers.

One day I got a postcard in the mail that said "The Church For People Who Don't Like Church." Well, that sounded perfect! I started going to the church and things started changing. Unlike most churches I had been to my life, I did not walk into a room of judgmental sneers. A beautiful woman in her 30s came up to me smiling, "Hey, how's it going?" She was the kind of person the 'normal', unchurched person like myself, would want to be friends with. Then more people who really started making me adjust my 'coolness' perception of churches in general, would introduce themselves to me. The place was set up exactly as I needed it. I didn't have to sit if I didn't want to; I didn't have to sing if I didn't want to; I could have even left half way through if I felt like it, but I never did. Somehow every word that came out of the pastor's mouth applied to my life at that point. In a room full of people, I felt like the words he was saying were directly for me, guiding me through the betrayal of my ex, the insecurities of my single life, and guiding me to my future choices.

I was teetering on faith, and my insomnia was as bad as it had ever been. There were several months that I only slept an hour or two every once in a while. At first, this seems cool when you want to go out and party or something, but I learned very quickly why your body needs sleep. My concentration would fail me as would almost every other aspect of my body. There were times I would feel like I was going to fall over from exhaustion but knew even if I did, I probably still wouldn't sleep. My ears would ring, and I had no idea why.

Finally, there came a night when I just started crying because I wanted it to stop, and I made a deal with God. "If you let me sleep, I promise you I will do whatever you want for the rest of my life." And I immediately fell asleep all night.

Well, that was one hell of a check to write! I woke up saying, "OK, well, that's what I'll be doing now." And I dedicated my life to following God. I'm not saying I was perfect or ever will be, but my goal was to try my hardest and live up to my promise.

With that, and a lot more sleep, I was on my way still rocking out to Guns and Roses.

# The Commitment-Phobe

I often joked about the fact that I've never got a tattoo because that is too much of a commitment. But with the idea of permanently branding my body when my concept of design is always changing, that's where the commitment-phobia stops… at least on the side that I bring to the relationship.

Several months passed, and one day I said to my friend, "Youngeon better get back here soon because I'm thinking about taking Army Boy up on his invitation to go visit him in Alabama." This was one of the first bizarre premonitions that I had about the Youngeon. Sure enough, I got a call on the phone about a week later.

"I got a new bike. Come out your front door." When I walked out front, the Youngeon was sitting on a silver Yamaha motorcycle, proud of his new purchase. I couldn't help but to laugh. We started talking, and he told me he just couldn't get me out of his mind. We sat on my bed for what seemed like hours when he went into an elaborate analogy of how I was like this perfect apple that he just needed to take a bite of. He stated that he didn't know why we couldn't try to have a relationship, and that he wanted to just do it.

We spent time together for a few weeks. Then one day he told me he wanted to go hang out with some girl who also had a bike. After stating that it seemed like a date, he disappeared on the same day he was supposed to hang out with her. The next day he came to my house with tears in his eyes and said, "I can't do it." He left my life again and I was heartbroken.

I can't say I learned a lot from this time around with Youngeon, but I did find that there was something wonderful about hearing that the person you cared so much about reciprocates those feelings. However, confusion is the only thing you'll be left with when a man treats you like an open door policy.

## Signs You Are Dating a Commitment-phobe

- They are very charming when they're around, but completely missing when they leave your house.

- They will remain silent or change topics if you start talking about the relationship.

- They don't spend the night with you.

- They call you an exercise bike or other piece of gym equipment.

- You have no plans that are too far into the future.

- Six months down the road, he's still introducing you as his "Friend."

- You still haven't meet the parents.

- Will not show affection in public.

- He thinks you should still "Date other people."

## Final Thoughts on Dating a Commitment-phobe

As amazing as the commitment-phobe might seem at first, if people don't want a relationship, it's better to not get into one with them. Unfortunately, some have no clue if they want to be in one or not, but if they're smart enough to know they don't want one, then don't push them. People who don't want to be in a relationship act like single people while still in a relationship and will be devastating to people who want a real commitment.

# Like a Brother

From the first glance to first exchange of phone numbers and that first date, each single person anticipates for first kiss where we will know if this is our soul mate, or something else…

I spent a lot of time at the gym. While most people these days use this venue for their Facebook photo ops or to wear completely inappropriate clothing to work out in, on the chance of meeting someone special, I've always been very serious about staying fit. Even though I'd look like I just rolled out of bed every time I walked into that place with no makeup on, there was a guy at the front desk at 24 Hour Fitness who would talk to me every time I came through the door. We'd make jokes and come up with horrible pickup lines. All my girlfriends called him "24". I could not put my finger on what it was about him. We seemed to immediately understand each other's demented humor. I gave him my number, but he wouldn't call. He wasn't the aggressive type that texted that night. A few days later, I found out he wasn't the 'play by the rules' type of waiting the two days. Since I saw him every time I went to the gym, it was inevitable that I was going to see him. When I did, I said, "Hey, there's an expiration on that number I gave you, and your time is running out." He started laughing and called me a day later.

We hung out one night and realized we had a lot of things in common when it came to our families. Neither one of us really had anyone blood-related that we could count on. By this time, after my divorce, I'd only hear from my father once every few months even though he lived twenty minutes away, and my mother was still out of the country. Both of us were running through this world figuring out what was right and wrong by trial and error, and both of us were constantly screwing up. That night things normally progressed. We kissed a little, but we could both tell things seemed weird and neither of us could put our fingers on it. I remember him leaving and all of a sudden it turned into that awkward hug like we both had Barbie arms and couldn't find how to wrap our arms around each other.

We didn't talk for several months and continued the uncomfortable interactions when we saw each other at the gym. Neither of us could define what the uneasiness was that happened that night.   I can't remember who figured it out first, but we eventually talked about and agreed that when we kissed it was like kissing a sibling and it should not have happened.   From that point forward, "24" became my brother. Although not blood related, we became each other's sole person who we could rely on in our crazy dating adventures.

## Signs You're Dating a Man Who's Like a Brother:

- Don't worry, you'll know when you kiss him!

## Final Thoughts on Dating a Man Who's Like a Brother

In the dating scene, you can get in the habit of sizing up everyone you meet to see if they're your perfect match, or list on a red paper, that you're looking for. Sometimes, if you remove the "significant other" stipulations from the mix, you'll discover that the person is meant to be something different in your life, but equally as important.

# The Game Player

Whether you don't have a clue, are always saying "Sorry," are great at kicking some balls, or going directly to jail, life is full of games. In sports, game playing is necessary, in business it can make or break success, but in relationships, when people start playing games it's questionable if anyone is a winner.

I could not get the Youngeon out of my head, and it was driving me nuts. Several months after our last encounter, I called him and told him that he was going to need to do something worse than what he did to me because I could not get him out of my mind. I'm not sure if he was trying to, or it just happened, but this is exactly what he did. By this point, my heart no longer cared. I was craving that feeling that I got when I was with him, the feeling that felt like another person was right. Even then, I still knew it was only a matter of time until the next disappearing act and I would be left in withdrawals again.

He said he was excited to hear from me and came over to my house. This was the first and only time I saw Kavic, my dog, do something completely unexplainable to a man I dated. Although my hundred-pound dog had the instinct in his blood to be a vicious killer, he had never acted out on a human before. He had never acted out on the Youngeon until this day. I looked out the window to see the Youngeon frozen, wide-eyed looking at Kavic who was hunched over snarling at him. This was the time I realized the truth behind people saying that animals know if a person is good or not. "The dogs always know." I broke Kavic from his stance, everyone snapped out of it and we went inside.

I heard familiar talk that day about wanting to be together and things were starting to look like a real relationship with us. After a few days I was so excited when he showed up at my house with a little pink helmet and saying he got it just for me to ride on his motorcycle with him. We went driving all over the city on the bike to watch fireworks on the Fourth of July. However, things started drifting into their old familiar ways with him when several days later he claimed that the bike helmet was not mine, but a helmet he had bought for "any girl." On Sunday morning I whispered in his ear, "I love you." He stood up, looked at me and said, "You just date the wrong men." I had been told this phrase by people a million times, but never from the man I was dating. All I could respond with was, "Why are you being one of them?" He hesitated at the door, but then he was gone, girl's helmet and all.

Months later, I found a MySpace account for him, which was strange because he said that he had never heard of MySpace. His profile revealed several rendezvous' between him and a seventeen-year-old girl during the time we had been dating. I guess that mystery was solved.

In the past, I lost a man I loved because he never knew, I don't regret telling the Youngeon that I loved him. Finding a reason as to why this person was in my life turned out to be a lot more complicated than I'd find out any time soon.

At this point, I realized how hurtful it could be to see betrayal played out against you on a social media account. I deleted my page and never wanted to see anyone I cared about actively deceiving me again. I obviously got another account, and about eight accounts on various sites all over the internet since then, but I never approached relationships and social media in the same way. I made it a practice to just not look at a profile that brings up negative feelings again.

Although I would rarely spend time on any man's social media pages, whether MySpace, Twitter, Facebook, whatever, if I saw something strange going on online and they couldn't give me a viable reason, I'd leave the situation.

## Signs You're Dating a Game Player:

- Their stories just don't add up.

- They love to play chase and will leave you for the sole reason that they want you to chase them or will only give you attention you need when you start ignoring them.

- They'll try to make you jealous by flirting with other people.

- They keep tabs on the relationship, "Well, you hurt me here, so I owe you this."

- They will disappear.

- Their feelings are hot and cold – One day it's nothing but XOXO text messages, the next he's taking his "Girl's Helmet" for the road.

- They will change topics if confronted with something that blows the whole game.

- You overhear a conversation with him and his boys and the word "bet" comes up.

- You still see them flirting with people online.

## Final Thoughts on Dating a Game Player

I've never been someone who plays games in relationships and have always been extremely straight-forward. Because of this approach, I've noticed a hypocrisy in men when it comes to game players. I've heard my entire life how men just can't handle girls who "cause drama" or "play games." However, once they get together with someone who has better things to do with her time, suddenly they don't know how to act. They start playing their own games in the relationship to the point where they destroy it. Then, months later, you'll see them hooked up with a girl that everyone in town calls a psychopath.

# The Clueless Man

You're going to find people out in the dating pool who are so wrong that they're like a big man in a Speedo. There's another "Wrong Man" who, on paper, seems to be Mr. Right, but a few interactions in, you find they are absolutely clueless.

People are changing all the time and whether single or in a relationship, you can't say that you're the same person you were two years ago as you were five or even twenty years ago! I have even dated Wrong Men where I was convinced their personality changed by the minute. Through the years Army Boy had carried this admiration of me, the girl he never knew in high school, and he was never shy about telling me. Though I was definitely not that girl in high school, he was so persistent on keeping up with me, I wanted to see if there was really something there.

He had been inviting me to Alabama since I met him and I finally took him up on it. I'm not sure if it was just to take my mind off of Youngeon but I was on my way. Although we had a fun night when we met at our high school reunion, I had no idea what I was in for and he obviously had no idea what to do once I got there.

I didn't think it was possible for a place to have more rain than Portland, Oregon, but, from what I could see, it seemed as though this town just saved up all its moisture in the air and spit it out in one multi-day storm that would wash out the entire city. This was exactly the few days that I spent here.

He had just bought a house but overlooked one important factor, furniture. There was no bed, no television sets, nothing. I'm not sure the strategy most men have for impressing girls with their house, but usually furniture is part of the deal.

Going out to eat, there was some casual small talk, but I found myself in this cycle of asking a question, getting a one or two word response, then moving on to the next question. I saw a confederate flag outside the window and had to ask, "What's up with that?" All of a sudden the floodgates opened and his opinion of racists spread all over our meal. Finally, some content to the conversation and an opinion I could admire. We continued to talk while we bought some furniture and the occasional statement of how I was the greatest thing to him in high school continued to come up. I think what had been going on with him was that he couldn't talk to me like a normal person because he had worked up some delusional "Dream Girl" in his head.

We went into a city with a good-sized group of his friends where our small talk turned to him ignoring proceeded to ignore me as he hung out with his friends. At this point, I started to think this was his default behavior for how he treated girls, but I didn't fly half way across the country for that. I went out on the dance floor and was joined by one of his friends. We were having a great time until I looked over to see the irritated Army Boy leaning against the wall.

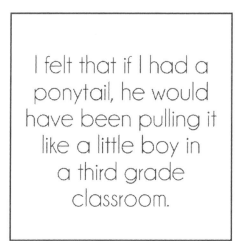

I felt that if I had a ponytail, he would have been pulling it like a little boy in a third grade classroom.

The next night we went to the bar where all the locals hung out and his misinterpretation of how a girl should be treated continued. I felt that if I had a ponytail, he would have been pulling it like a little boy in a third grade classroom. I sat in a corner by myself for the entire night with the look on my face of "You've got to be kidding me!"

Day three came, and as he left me in his empty house and went to his friend's place to play video games, I decided to take matters into my own hands. I took the car and went back to the locals bar. Several people were there from the night before and I sat next to them at the bar. One guy, John, started talking to me. "I saw you here last night. That guy you were here with was a jerk." I proceeded to tell the story of how I had flown there from

Oregon and have been basically been ignored ever since. Within about fifteen minutes all the locals and I were toasting at the bar and having a great time! Even the big local oaf, Junior, was running over giving me big hugs.

After a few hours, my phone rang.

> Army Boy: "Where are you?"
> Me: "I'm at the bar."
> Army Boy: "Where's my car?"
> Me: "It's at the bar."
> Army Boy: "Who are you with?"
> Me: "My friend John."
> Army Boy: "OK I'm coming down."

At this point everyone at the bar knew exactly what was going on. Army Boy and his friend came into the bar. This time it was my turn to ignore. I just continued to joke around with my new friends until Army Boy got up and went to the bathroom. John and Junior followed close behind.

A few minutes later, that bathroom door came swinging open and Army Boy flew out of there pissed. He walked up to me and said, "We're leaving." So we headed for the door. I guess John and Junior went in there to mess with him saying things like, "Damn, that hot girl wants me so bad. If I had her in my life I'd never let that one get away." Army Boy was so livid he almost drove off the road that night.

The next day I headed home, to hopefully better weather and definitely a better dating situation.

## Signs You're Dating a Clueless Man

- They seem enamored with you when they talk about you, yet you find yourself wondering, "Does he even realize I'm in this room?" when with him.

- They're sitting in the driver's seat smiling blindly at you while you're outside of the car opening your own door.

- You're picking up the tab… again.

- He's more into the idea of "You" than the idea of "Us."

## Final Thoughts on Dating a Clueless Man

It's good to understand that even when a person puts you on a pedestal their whole life, they still might not have a clue how to treat a girl. Maybe the guy you're with has really great feelings for you but was never shown how to treat a woman. In these situations you really need to decide if you're willing to test the waters and spend the time to get some changes. I've had friends say, "You've just got to train guys!" And many of my friends have taken the time to do this and have relationships that work for them because of it. If you take this approach, you have to realize that some guys may never change the way they treat you and you might come to a point where you need to decide to walk away or just live with it. Me, I'm the type of girl who wants the quality I expect at the time of purchase and the only thing I would like to train is my dog.

# The Gigolo

Have you ever heard that fable of the turtle and the snake?  It's about a snake who needs a ride over the river and tells the turtle, "Hey, if you give me a ride over this river, I won't bite you." Halfway across the river, the disgusting snake bites the turtle which sentences them both to their deaths.  Before they die, the turtle asks, "Why would you bite me?" and the snake replies, "I'm a snake. It's in my nature."  I used to hate this fable because I think all these snakes walking around as humans should get it together, stop biting people, and stop excusing it as something they were born with.  But in this Wrong Man story, all I could do is be glad I knew this fable before deciding to take this snake over the water.

I had been flirting with a guy at the gym for several months.  We'd see each other all around town, lock eyes, and flash shy smiles at each other. It seemed as though we were both too nervous around each other to really talk much.  We'd talk at one point, get a tidbit of information about each other and then run off like little kids. Both of us were obviously coming up with ridiculous reasons to talk to each other.  A million times over, I'd have guys at the gym walk up to me with some horrible meditated pickup lines as if I had come there to be in their presence.  But he was the only one I would take my earphones out for when he approached.

One night when I was walking down the street with a group of my friends, past the back door of a club, and saw him pop out with a broom at the exact moment I walked by.  He came to a dead stop and watched me with dreamy eyes as I continued to walk down the street. I turned around when I got to the end of the block.  He was still standing there smiling at me and just waved.

Although there seemed to be a lot of intense flirting and seeing each other everywhere, things weren't what they seemed.  I was with a personal trainer one day doing sit-ups when he walked by.  When I just froze, the trainer said, "What are you doing here?  Why are you stopping?" I pointed out the guy, explaining how gorgeous he was, only to hear the trainer say, "Oh him? He's a stripper. All the male strippers work out here."

What!? My jaw dropped to the floor and my eyes were the size of a baseball. That was the last thing I saw coming. Thinking back to that night in the street, I realized that the club he was coming out of was the same one where they had a show called, "Men of Paradise." Suddenly, everything made sense. I went out to my car to see him load up his Escalade, which was the exact same car that all his stripper buddies had. I found out that each of these cars were bought for them by their older sugar mammas. In the following weeks, I'd tell this story to several different groups of friends. Not one, but two entire groups of women knew exactly who he was. Not only could they describe details of his body I had never seen, but they knew him by his 'animal' stage name.

Call me selfish, but I decided then and there that I didn't want to be dating someone of whom, at any point of time, a girl would be able to say, "Oh yeah, I saw your man's package last night."

## Signs You're Dating a Gigalo

- They want money from you.

- They drive an insanely expensive car they didn't pay for.

- They have shown one or more of your friends their penis.

- Most of the general public knows them by a stage name usually referencing an animal or an over-exaggerated adjective about their body parts.

## Final Thoughts on Dating a Gigalo

Once I asked a former female stripper straight up, "Do you think a stripper can realistically have a healthy, monogamous relationship while they're still stripper?" She said, "No." I think the key word here is "monogamous." Like I said in my chapter overviewing the "Wrong Men" in this book, what some people can't handle in relationships, others think is no big deal. At the end of the day, it's knowing what you will and will not accept in a relationship. Anything less than monogamy for me is a no-can-do.

# The Freeloader

In the developmental years of life, clearly it's great to have a parent, guardian, or someone financially supportive to teach them to be independent of those who raised them. However, too often in my single girl career, I would find men who just couldn't break their dependent approach to life and were looking towards me to fill the void of the person who would take care of them or the pocketbook that ceased to exist.

Popping up in the clubs from time to time was a guy my girlfriends and I called "Holister" strictly from his choice in clothing. He was quiet but would suddenly start break dancing on the dance floor. If you remember my red piece of paper, I love a guy who can dance. For months, we would see each other and had each other's number, but nothing happened. Then the day came along where he picked me up outside of a club. I don't mean in his car, I mean he literally picked me up by my waist and held me above him. Soon, we started dating.

He was quiet and sweet with bad-boy hobbies, but not the type that would break my heart. He had lived doing stunts on his motorcycle until a terrible accident he had several months before we met. Apparently, he had been driving his motorcycle down the freeway at 12 o'clock, meaning he had the front wheel almost directly over the back. The muffler caught on the ground and the bike flipped backwards over him. Going that fast, his body scraped on the pavement and ripped off his armor. That's the day he says he saw an angel as the bike missed his head by an inch. He had the same new-found life for God and excitement in his life. He definitely had me interested.

When we started dating, he had three jobs and what I thought were all functioning body parts. He didn't seem ambitious, per se, but at least he could hold his own. Then a few months into the relationship, the first red flag flew up at full mast. "Oh yea, my foot is broken. I never got it fixed." I mean, this wasn't like an oil change, how could this just be overlooked? For months he had hobbled around. The whole thing didn't make sense. He had health insurance, plus his mom had worked a deal out with the doctor to give him a discount. All I could figure is that no one was physically forcing him to get surgery. The fact that his foot was broken caused his performance at work to slowly suffer. Three jobs went down to two. Two turned into one. One turned into spending day in and day out at my house, distracting me from my work with his broken foot.

This went on for about six months with no sign of that foot ever being fixed. I mean, why should he? I provided such a great living situation where he didn't have to do anything except chill. Without a job, I was suddenly financially responsible for everything we did. I started feeling like I was no longer responsible for solely my life, but for his too. As sweet as he was, I couldn't do it. With Valentine's Day approaching, I only remembered the great memories of the holiday with Youngeon and realized my heart was not in this relationship. I broke up with him on my birthday, the week before Valentine's Day, which became a habit through the years.

A few days after our breakup, he went into surgery to get his foot fixed a little too late to save our relationship. I wasn't interested in supporting a man, acting as someone's mother, or being anyone's personal nurse. And, as sweet as the guy was, the whole thing was a pain in the … foot.

Sometimes a breakup is the best thing for a person. Some people get so comfortable with how things are that they don't even realize they are doing nothing about something so broken.

## Signs You're Dating a Freeloader

- They won't make decisions on their own.

- They won't pay for things.

- You find yourself not as attracted to them anymore.

- You're expecting your couch to have a fort on it any day now.

- Resentment builds.

- You'll start being addressed by "Mom… oh I mean,…"

## Final Thoughts on Dating a Freeloader

There are dependency issues and then there's someone who wants you to make every decision in his life for him. I'm not sure if it's that they just don't know what they want, or that they want someone else to make the hard calls so they don't have to take on the responsibility if anything ever goes wrong.

I have seen the freeloading aspect destroy so many relationships and generally leave the freeloader wondering what they had done wrong. A dear guy friend of mine was in a relationship with a Maxim model for several years. Somehow, he wasn't working at all. You could feel the tension between the two growing as the month's went on. For some reason or another, he wouldn't go get a job. Finally, one day, she broke up with him which turned into probably his biggest regret in life. It wasn't until then that he went out and started a very successful company.

I know woman are bursting that glass ceiling like a piñata at a sugar-crazed kid's party, but there shouldn't be an automatic assumption that all of the responsibilities of life should lie in one person's hands or the other. If your freeloader is around for too long, you'll find that those amazing qualities he used to have are replaced by resentment. Obviously, talking it through is step one. You may even want to set a time limit afterwards to determine how long you will wait for this to end. But keep in mind that the day might come where you need to take the "Loader" out of the equation and just set him "Free."

# God Might Not Want You to Be a Nun

For years, my weight fluctuated, but I tended to get heavier. Since I worked at home, I started what I called my own private "Ice Cream Socials" where I would eat ice cream during the day. I mean, what could be better than that? This amazing plan ended when I went to the doctor and found out I was thirty pounds heavier than my regular weight. Oops.

During the time of dating Holister, the pastor signed me up to run Hood to Coast with the church team even though I said "no." This was the first of many blessings in disguise. Hood to Coast is the longest relay in the world that stretches from Mt. Hood to the Oregon coast, 197 miles. Each team member ends up running about 15-20 miles throughout the course of a day-and-a-half so I had to figure out a way to do this.

I trained consistently for this since, before this point, I would struggle running even a mile. I had to get to the point where I could run seven-and-a-half miles with no problem. After training almost a year, I got my running up to par. But I also saw the other benefit. I lost all the weight I had put on from years of bad eating, my "Ice Cream Socials," and massive beer consumption. I was down to the weight I had been right out of high school and getting compliments from friends and family. With the boost in confidence, not to mention the ability to wear cute clothes, I found my self-worth increasing. It's funny how when you feel like you are providing a better "you" to a potential partner, you expect a lot more in return. So off I ran, literally, in life and my relationships looking for someone who could keep up. The whole thing showed me God's plan for everyone isn't to become reserved and shuffle people away into convents. God had another idea for me. It included getting in shape and running Hood to Coast three times through the years.

# The Man Racing to the Altar

Sometimes, when I walk down that candy isle, I see a huge box of Nerds and just think, "That is the best thing in the world. I need to buy it NOW!" Many times in my life, I have made that purchase commitment, eaten an entire six ounces of Nerds candy when I got home and sat up for hours that night sick out of my mind. I have yet to learn the restraint of portion control on that candy. Candy is one thing, but jumping into relationships as you would a quick candy isle purchase might leave you nothing but buyer's remorse.

Through some old high school friends, I met a man who had been divorced two months prior. He was full of smiles and seemed to be very excited about life. It seemed very different from the effects of my divorce or anyone else's I'd seen. He'd joke around about how his ex left him for her old boyfriend, then move on to the next topic. Ever the busybody, this divorcee was on to the next task on his To-Do list and I had no idea I was one of the check boxes.

He had a good job, check. Paid his own bills, check. Did not live with his parents, check. And had a strategy as to how he was going to get where he needed to go in life and no one was going to stop him. Things moved very fast with us going from flirting to ultra-serious without me ever getting a chance to consult that feeling deep down that it was right. We were going from first date

This divorcee was on to the next task on his To-Do list and I had no idea I was one of the check boxes.

to spending all our time together to taking disastrous road trips, and I could not find the brakes!

I must have known that something was very wrong when five months down the road I had not slept with him. However, this did not stop his plans. After he put together an excel spreadsheet of our joint finances, he decided that living together would be the best idea. With great hesitation I said Ok. Slowly, things from his house were moving into mine. I felt them creeping into my space I had built in the several years since my divorce. With every piece of clothing or BBQ equipment that came in my anxiety rose. While rearranging one of my drawers, he found one of the Youngeons belongings and got mad. I had no idea it was still in the house, but then he swiftly threw it away. I knew something was very wrong when I wanted the Youngeons article out of the garbage and his stuff out. A day or two passed, and right as things started to settle, a freezer was delivered to my house and I flipped out. It was too much and it didn't feel right! We were pushing something when he didn't fit half of what I was looking for in a man. I told him that we had to end it right then and there.

He was very civil about the breakup and moved his things out. Of course, like all the others, he was attempting to leave a few things there to have a reason to come back. At this time, I saw a picture of his ex-wife. She looked identical to me. Shortly after, he married another woman who also did.

This guy wasn't looking for the same things I was in a relationship. I wanted the whole shebang of love, magic, and a partner for life. I wanted to find that match from my red piece of paper. I'm pretty sure he was just looking to fill the spot and move on to the next task at hand.

## Signs You Are Dating a Man Racing to the Altar

- Their ex is still living at his house.

- They call you by the wrong name.

- They're laying out joint finances.

- They have shipped large appliances to your house.

- Their overnight bag has turned into half of your closet.

- He starts calling you "Wifey" after a week.


## Final Thoughts on Dating a Man Racing to the Altar

I have dated people where both of us have felt like our feelings were moving too quickly. But, as far as the aspects to a relationship, our heads could conquer our racing hearts and lay the ground work of what was healthy and what wasn't. On the other side of the coin, a friend of mine's parents got married two weeks after they met and are still married 40 years later. I think you have to feel out every situation differently on how fast to take things. I think you'll know the right comfort level for you and you have to follow it. If you are really the one important person that someone has been waiting for, then they will go at the speed you need.

# Roid Rage Guy

Girls put their bodies through the most obnoxious nightmares from birth control to weight loss, to skin care, to hair removal. The list goes on! But I have yet to see any of these things that a woman does to herself make a girl act half as crazy as a guy on steroids.

I started really hitting the club scene in Portland, and in a small town, you start to know everyone. However, just because you know someone at a nightclub does not mean you know them well, let alone their psychological history. A very buff guy I met through the club scene and I started to hang out one weekend outside of the clubs. He was very quiet at first, but the hints of randomly screaming on the phone at his best friends were only a taste test as to where this was headed.

At first, I thought he must have been joking with his buddies when every time he picked up the phone he started screaming demands. One night, we went on a walk down the street. I thought maybe it would be something romantic, but then he seemed determined to get somewhere. We walked down the street to some girl's house where he started getting angry about the fact that his friend's car was out front. The walk home was filled with the sound of an angry phone call to his friend. Seemed more like a jealous marriage than a friendship with two guys. One night we went to a UFC fight. I got the first tip-off from some friends that it looked as though he was on steroids. This started to make sense. It wasn't long until his roid rage was aimed at me. However, I had done crazy before, and I wasn't interested in it again. I called it off and prayed he'd take the hint.

Sure enough, when I started ignoring his phone calls, all of my phone lines started blowing up. I started to wonder if he had found my first love's screenplay and interpreted it as a "How To" guide. He obsessively called for days leaving threats on my voicemail until I changed my number and called the cops. The female cop I talked to had dealt with a lot of girls who made up situations to try to get their significant other in trouble, so she nonchalantly said she'd give him a call assuming I was full of it. Within ten minutes the cop called me back and stated, "This man is crazy! He just started yelling at me. And when I told him that if a girl changes her number that's a sign that it's over, he said, 'Well everyone changes their number!' At the cop's request, I installed an alarm system in my house. She asked me to finish one last thing with him that he was claiming was all he needed from me.

In further proof that every man will leave something at your house to see you again, this guy demanded that I give back a pickle jar that was his grandmother's that he conveniently left in my fridge. I stated I'd bring it to him. I'm sure he thought I'd show up alone, but after Crazy Number One back in college, I wasn't going to give him anything he wanted. I brought one of my male friends with me and handed him his empty pickle jar. I had nothing more to say.

I'd see him at clubs from time to time where he would chase me down, push me in the back and be escorted out by security. After changing my club rotation he soon couldn't find me at all. He'd then run into my friends from time to time, corner them and tell them whatever delusional story was in his head about me.

Through the years, I'd hear similar stories about him harassing other girls. Then the day came when I had to work at an event at a club, and we were stuck right next to each other while getting inside. I looked at him and said, "This is what's going to happen right now. I'll hook you up and get you into this club right now, but you will forever stay the hell away from me and never talk about me again to anyone." Done. It was over. We both held our part of the deal.

Crazy can be dealt with, and if you learn the process once, you'll remember it forever. Don't give them anything to feed their delusions and walk the other way. State things clearly, leave the situation completely, and get the cops involved if need be. No matter what, always be leery of anyone who is overly attached to a pickle jar.

## Signs You Are Dating a Roid Rage Guy

- They sporadically yell at you, their friends and family.

- "No" is not something they can hear.

- They call obsessively.

- They threaten you.

- They find deep meaning in everyday household items and use them to maintain contact with you.

- Mood swings.

- Vials and Syringes in the bathroom.

- Veins bulging out of their neck.

- Snapping at everyone all the time... even the innocent little girl at a lemonade stand.

## Final Thoughts on Dating a Roid Rage Guy

Most times I have known people to use steroids, they have told me they use them. I think they do so because they are a somewhat socially acceptable drug? However, their reactions while on it are just as bad if not worse than some of the illegal drugs I've seen people do as far as how they treat other people. If you start dating someone and he openly tell you he takes steroids, just watch for the behavior and if things heat up with him, run, because rarely have I seen a really buff guy actually be able to run very far.

# Success in Business

My business had grown with the changes in marketing from graphic design to web design, but I would pray time and time again for a more steady income without all the ups and downs. A year prior, I had gone to Vegas with a girlfriend and I had an idea in my head that would not escape me. I wanted to create an automated system where people could put their own names on the list at night clubs. When an idea is in my head for that long, I realize it is God telling me I had to do something. It was the same with this book. However, it never made sense to me why God would want me on a path that was so involved in nightlife, but I did it all the same. And this was the birth of a website I called my baby, AllClubVIP.com.

Soon, I met photographers at the clubs who would be taking pictures and then you'd never see them again. I said, "Why don't you put them on my website so people can get their pictures?" and we were rolling. Within a few months, it had numbers that I had never seen before with everyone in town visiting it on a weekly basis. Knowing everything I knew about marketing, I went to clubs with packages and we were all getting paid.

> This business was transforming me and my life quickly for my next big move and the man who might be able to handle them.

I still struggled with whether or not I was doing the right thing with the site. I introduced it to some ladies in a Bible study class I was in to see what they thought. Each of them created profiles on the site and looked around until we met at our next study. They searched through every user and came back appalled at a few of the members on the site because of statements like "I'll make any man unfaithful."

They thought the site was catering to nothing but heathens and their initial suggestion was that I should shut the site down.

Completely devastated and panicking that I might have misinterpreted God's plan for me, I went out to a club that night that had approximately the same capacity as the number of members on my site at the time and started looking around. I looked at every person there and thought about what must have brought them to the club that night. Some were celebrating, others were just looking to have some fun, and some, similar to what my life had been, were drinking to escape whatever pain was going on in their life. Sure, some were there with bad intentions, but that large of a percentage of people are not bad people. Maybe these people already had God in their life. Or maybe they'd been curious but always turned away because of attitudes like those of the women in my Bible study. I went back to the group with what I thought.

The Bible study girls took a step back and one of them said, "You're right, I feel like a hypocrite. I've been raised my entire life in the church, being taught to accept others and the first sign of people outside the church I see, I judge them." That woman was my pastor's wife. A few months later, she and her husband started an amazing nonprofit organization that helped people in need by repairing their houses while sharing with them about God. I can't help but to think that this experience with All Club lead them to branch out to help people who would have been previously outside of their comfort zone.

All Club stayed up for several years and became my sole source of income. When people acted like scum on the site, or offended others, I stepped up and sent them a note telling them to clean their profile or get off the site. Having high ethical standards, even in a dark industry, was more important than pleasing anyone.

The years with All Club weren't just steps, they were a flight of stairs I had to leap up to get where I needed to be for what was coming in my future. It opened my mind to get me ready for the acceptance I needed to have for people in my coming career moves, but also showed me the shadiest of the shady people in business. My public image went from being some no-body at the club to being approached by random people walking down the street asking me to accept their friend requests. Photo by photo, this business was transforming me and my life quickly for my next big move and the man who might be able to handle them.

# The Men You'll Meet Online Dating

Every single person has got to try online dating at least once and many have great success. You meet a ton of people who at least can afford a subscription, who are ready to date, and are intelligent enough to turn on a computer. After weeding through the profiles of outdated, 100-pound lighter profile pictures, and dates who have reeled you in with their slightly exaggerated selection of "characteristics" from the drop box options, you may actually click on that future love of your life. However, I had three experiences with online dating that were fun, but it was questionable if Wi-Fi was really the only connection in the situation.

My first date was with a guy who took me to eat Vietnamese food. He seemed very exciting and fun to be with. We talked about all kinds of topics and seemed to get along all the way around. I thought he was very handsome, but in the end it showed that he still didn't believe it.

We started talking about high school. He had gone to the public school that I would have gone to and happened to be in the same classes as my First Love. He, like me, was not the same person he was back then. Apparently he had been obese in high school and worked hard through the years to lose the weight. It also turned out that he knew my First Love from those days and my ex was anything but kind to him. Just knowing that I had dated someone who used to make fun of him in high school made all his insecurities about his weight come back and I never heard from him again.

The next guy I dated, I called the "Match.com Pimp." I'm pretty sure he had some kind of executive membership or something. On the date he explained how much Match rocked because he could be anywhere in the world and if he was bored one night, BAM! Date for the night. I'm completely convinced this guy had his next month laid out with dates from Match. He was successful, having a good time and knew exactly what to do to impress the ladies. We went out for steak bites and jumped in his Camaro to cruise around. He would speed up the hill and fishtail out into multiple 360s. As impressed as I was, I couldn't help but think he's doing this every night. And, if I don't work out, he'll just move on to the next profile.

The third guy I went out with was very sweet and attractive, but he was a country boy, which was very different for me. He had the dangerous timing of asking me out close to my birthday which had been detrimental in the past. It turned out he lived on the same property in the country as his parents. Like many of the people in online dating he was ready to settle down, and he meant now. I, on the other hand, was still looking for exactly what felt right without the pressure of settling down immediately. However, I decided to give him a shot and I headed to his house to go out near his neck of the woods.

This was only our second date, so I was not prepared for what happened next. I walked into the living room to find that he had baked a dozen cupcakes with "Happy Birthday" written on them and arranged them in a heart around a dozen roses and several gifts. If this was the right guy, I would have been ecstatic, but it was too soon and I freaked out. This was the second time I ended things with a man on my birthday.

This wasn't my last attempt at online dating, but I disconnected for awhile and counted on life to set me up rather than computer algorithms.

## Signs You Are Dating the Men You Met Online

- Your initial impression of them was a profile picture.

## Final Thoughts on Dating the Men You Met Online

I have had several friends who have had great success in meeting their perfect match online. A few even have got married! On the other side, I've had friends who have had similar situations to mine. The great thing about online dating is that everyone seems to be at a place where they want to settle down. The ones who don't are very blatant in their initial emails about their borderline prostitution approaches. You can find some great, successful people on there who just can't find the time to date. I think one of the biggest things you have to look out for with online dating is meeting a person who thought he was ready for a relationship, but deep down really wasn't.

# The Emotional Drainer

No matter what ups and downs I've had in my life, I like to think that if I looked at a graph of my progression in life it has always been going up through the years. I've had my share of dips here and there, and not just the ones I've dated, but overall I keep striving to become a better person. I have been very grateful for the people who have stuck by me even when going through the hard times, and those friendships are the ones I consider the truest. However, every once in a while, you might have someone pop into your life who will use you to help brush himself off only to leave you covered in the dirt.

It started snowing that year and, looking down on my porch, I saw shoe prints one night. I got a strange feeling looking at them, but I still carried on with my plans by going over to my friend's house. Being the MySpace addicts that we were, I logged into my account and my heart dropped.

The Youngeon had messaged me saying that he stopped by that day. It had been years since I'd seen him, and he wanted to talk. The next day he came over after work. Something seemed different about him, almost sad, but I was just happy to have him around so I welcomed him with open arms. His nice Trooper was replaced by a beat up old truck and there were other slight but odd differences about him, but I couldn't place a finger on it. We went to dinner where he stated that I was someone who he could always talk to and he needed that, although nothing he said seemed to be what was on his mind. We snuggled on the couch together, but it never went to that physical place that our relationship started out with this time around. I told him the intimate details of the ups and downs of the last few years and he would squeeze me with concern any time I had a painful story. I had dated several people since the last time I had seen him, and I was amazed that he still felt like the only one I could really talk to.

I wasn't looking for a relationship with him this quickly and no pain that I had from his disappearance after I told him I loved him was discussed. There wasn't enough time to. I asked him to dinner on that Sunday, and he never showed. After I left a message on his voicemail begging for some kind of reasoning, he called me and told me that he had been dating a girl that he went back to.

I had to accept that some girl out there was taking him down, making him miserable, and I was the girl he would could come back to when it was time to pick up the pieces.

## Signs You Are Dating an Emotional Drainer

- They always need something from you.

- There is no long term commitment.

- They can't stop talking about the negative things in their life.

- They have no interest in what is going on in your life.

## Final Thoughts on Dating an Emotional Drainer

Relationships are all about support-two people who support each other in the ups and downs of life. The ideal partner is someone who can provide a soft place to land in a time of need. However, sometimes we get caught up in our desires for a healthy relationship and disregard the fact that only one person in the situation is bracing the other's fall.

# It's Never Too Late to Be a Good Parent

From break up to break up, I used to joke with people that I was a professional "Bailer" from the ways I'd just walk away from a horrible relationship never to be seen again. But, for every pro, there is still someone better, and that would be my mother, the Queen of the Bail when it came to her Wrong Man. For twenty-five years she had been married to my father, and she was more than lost when the divorce came around. Who was she if she wasn't in this relationship? During a break up some people just stop going to the same coffee shops their ex is at, some might change their church. My mom changed her life and her friends and bailed the country! She landed her dream job as a librarian for the military which sent her off, bouncing around the world, dealing with her own "Wrong Man" breakup. No story in the world is a better example than hers that sometimes distance and time is the best solution for the important relationships in your life and the secrets to happiness.

> "Do you know what a body shot is?" started a conversation when she was around 58.

My mom is in love with books, but the similarity to a librarian stops there. The reading part of the hiring process made sense to me when she got this job, but I always thought, "She is one of the most talkative people on the planet. How in the heck did she get this job? She'll have to kick herself out of that library!" But she got the job and she was awesome at it. Through living in three continents, four countries, six different cities, and God knows how many million road trips, she spent ten plus years figuring out who she was without that man by her side. She'd call me when she could and the calls got more frequent. Traits of her personality started shining through that showed me that this was definitely my mother, traits that seemed to have been lost so long ago. "Do you know what a body shot is?" started a conversation when she was around 58. This person started to make more sense to me. She got to the point where she absolutely loved her life and the things she did. She got to travel the world, which she never would have done otherwise. She made true friends and took on things that people her age never would have, like paragliding in Turkey.

Most importantly, she figured out the best way to be a good mom and put in the time to be part of my life despite the distance. My mom and my relationship grew to be something that I had always needed from a family member and gave me a much needed stable ground on the shakiness of my dating life. We were two "happening" single ladies on the market and even though were on other sides of the planet, nothing was going to stop us!

# Your Best Friend

In the world of singles asking themselves, "How am I going to meet the right person?" there is usually that one person who always pops in your head who can take the whole aspect of having to bring another unknown into your life to solve your single status blues. This person has been there time and time again, runs in your social circles, shares everything with you, knows your ups and downs and still puts up with your crap. With the timeless question from When Harry Met Sally of whether or not a man and woman can just "be friends" lurking over their heads, many singles throw in the towel to the constant romantic tension and start dating their best friend, or in some cases, their next Wrong Man.

I've attempted to date someone I considered to be my best guy friend twice and a few months after Youngeon left my life again, my life faced that option. I never thought another connection like the one I had to Youngeon was possible again, but I knew I was more than happy with my best guy friend. He knew everything about me, what I was all about in relationships, and I knew the same about him. Everyone I told about him would ring the phrase, "Well you know, the best relationships start out as friends."

Our entire group of friends started getting disgusted by our constant picking and flirting with each other. One winter day, we were all up at the ski lodge we were all sitting around the table where my friend grabbed my hand and started writing "LOS..." and I pulled my hand away. "Are you trying to say that you LOVE me!!??" That is so cute!!" The conversation went back and forth for awhile and his final claim was, "No, I was saying I Losi You." For a long time, "I losi you" was our key phrase in the group.

The flirting and eye rolling from our friends continued for several months until he was transferred to Hawaii for work. We hit the town one last time before he left and the tension between us was ridiculous. However, soon he was gone. Ever the "friend of convenience," one of my girlfriends took this as an opportunity to book a trip to Hawaii stating that I needed to go, too. At first I told her that I didn't think it was a good idea because it seemed as though my guy friend and I might not be able to keep it just friends for too much longer. After basically sitting me at her computer pressing "Confirm" for me, my friend convinced me to go and conveniently made it so there was no other place for me to sleep at his house but his bed.

It was an amazing time in such a beautiful place. My girl friend, however, didn't realize how disgusted she'd get by my friend and my flirting. It appeared as though she went through every means possible to get in between my best guy friend and I. She even went so far as to strip down to her underwear and prance around in front of him. Needless to say, this ended our friendship. She continued with this approach to get his attention for the rest of the week and I just threw up my hands like "Go ahead!" But he didn't cave. In fact, this was the first man I had ever dated that made it a point to show me that I was more important than another girl. When I walked off from the group to sit on the wall overlooking the ocean, he followed me. It was very obvious I was irritated, then… we started talking. We made it clear to each other that we both had feelings towards each other, but the timing was wrong since he had just been transferred out of state. After an intense, what-could-have-been moment, we went inside the bar.

I didn't really want to hang out with that girlfriend of mine anymore, so I started running around the bar doing my own thing. Dabbling again with drinking too much, at one point I helped convince a girl in the bathroom to let us cut her shirt up. This was already an ugly fashion at the time, but for some reason, alcohol had convinced me I could make all the difference. I came out of the bathroom to the group who had wondered where I went with my new piece of art, this girl's shirt. My guy friend started cracking up, grabbed my face, kissed me and said, "Let's do this." That was that!

I'd fly out there several times, or he'd come to see me and we were a great couple. We always had fun and joked around. He wouldn't dream of throwing another girl in my face. And we already had all the same friends. A strange thing happens when you start dating your best friend. For so long, all you'd seen them as is your friend. They've been that person to confide in about your relationships or lack-there-of. You have that goofy, almost boundary-free relationship where you can just be yourselves and not worry too much because, hey, you're not going home with him! Once you cross that line with your best friend into becoming a relationship, suddenly you see the other side of a person. It's like both people try to squeeze their 'relationship self' into a situation that is usually with someone who doesn't know anything about them. In successful attempts, the best friends as single people mesh pretty nicely with their relationship selves. This Hawaii love affair was pretty close to that, but with every Jimmy Buffet song and Lava Mama drank, other problems were arising.

> Your best friend may or may not be the person you end up dating, but in the best relationships, the person you date ends up being your best friend.

The time came that I had to go back home, which became the reoccurring theme of our relationship. I'd fly out there, or he would fly home for a week or so only to leave again. It never seemed real to me. At first, his work said that he would only be out there for a few months, but three turned to six and then he was lined up to be out there the rest of the year. My patience wore thin and his frustration at work became too great. We ended up fighting all the time. Finally, one fight ended it all on both of our parts when he said, "You need to stop putting all your faith in God and just do what needs to be done in life." After years of failure from putting my faith in my own life strategy, I decided that having faith in God was really a better plan, so we called it a day. I guess I chose my faith over that relationship.

All of a sudden I was lost. In other breakups, I had my friend's shoulder to cry on, but what was I supposed to do when he was gone? Since the majority of our friends were guys following the 'bro code' the guys soon stopped being friends with me as well. At the time, I thought I had the most amazing friends in the world, but this situation showed me that even in tight circles, you'll soon find which friendships are real and which are fake.

When it comes to dating your best friend, you have a 50/50 chance of things working out well. In the two times I did it, this case was the more positive of my experiences.

## Signs You Are Dating Your Best Friend

- You were friends before you started dating!

## Final Thoughts on Dating Your Best Friend

Call me a gambler, but I think taking the chance to date your best friend is worth the shot. You already know what crap they will give you long before you'd have to find out otherwise. Your best friend may or may not be the person you end up dating, but in the best relationships, the person you date ends up being your best friend.

# What Dolly Parton Has To Do With Your Rotting Eggs

Hey men, guess what? Your junk is going nowhere! Men are blessed with the ever-producing sperm where they can wake up at Hugh Hefner's age and decide, "Hey, I want to have a kid!" This can happen whether or not they have ten young blondes on their side or not. Women are not that lucky and once you hit that big 3-Oh, the pressure is on. Every woman starts calculating in their head at this point, "OK, I need to allow this many months for getting to know the guy, this many years for dating, wedding planning takes at least a year, etc." and the final total puts you at 85 years old when you're at that point you can have a kid. This is where I was.

I had always wanted kids, but decided that I shouldn't have contributed to the procreation of the men I had dated. The pressure really started to build up and became so depressing thinking about the ever disappointing genes that are floating around in the dating pool. God knows I had made excuses for men before as to how they were so great and wonderful, but this added stress to wrap up the baby plan seemed to just make things more ridiculous. Dates turned into fatherhood trials and I'd definitely ditch guys quicker if I didn't think they could make the cut. Then one day I saw the True Hollywood Story of Dolly Parton.

Men and women would both agree that Dolly Parton had amazing God-given assets for motherhood, but I was surprised to find out she never had kids. In the special, she explained how it just didn't happen with how busy she had always been. She had a loving husband for most of her life and iconic career, but the kids didn't happen. She explained how she just treated every child as her own and this is what led her to build her amusement park Dolly World. Suddenly, my own pressure of having kids was lifted. This woman, who will go down history as one of the most business savvy, entertaining icons of the century, did not have kids. Instead of being bitter or resentful, she found ways to fulfill mothering desires by taking on the kids of the world as her own and is genuinely a happy person. Definitely not a bad plan.

I'm not saying it still might not happen for me, I'm saying that I got to the point where I was OK if it doesn't, thanks to Ms. Parton.

# The Man Who Prefers the "Wrong Girls"

Unfortunately, we've gotten in our society to the place where men will scrape the bottom of the barrel claiming it is "Love" for the sole fact that this person is the one person on the planet that they can look at and say, "I treat people like crap, but at least I'm better than the girl I date." I call this when a man decides to "Take out the Trash."

I guess I couldn't hide the feelings of losing my best friend well when people would come up to me at clubs and mention, "Hey, you're the girl from All Club who always looks sad in pictures." I was kind of aimlessly wandering through life again, doing what needed to be done with a lot less excitement. Then one night I was set into some kind of cosmic spin when Youngeon found me at a club.

It had almost been a year since I had seen him and I couldn't understand why he was following me around one random night. Wasn't he with some girl? Why did he keep wanting to rip my heart out? What was this guy on? As much as I would try to avoid him, he would be there smiling at me, though his last interaction with me gave me no reason to smile back at him. He finally came up and held my hand with no words. So I started talking to him. "What?" We talked for a while about where we were in life. He explained how he was in medical school now and when I asked what made him start doing that he proclaimed, "So I can take care of you." The words sounded sweet, but only as sweet as a huge lollipop in a kid's hand before being ripped out right before he gets a taste. One of my girlfriends walked up and stated, "Oh no, not again! You're not going to do this again," and he walked out of the club and my life. Yet again.

I had had it with this man treating me like I was some kind of revolving door! I needed answers from this guy and I wasn't going to rest until I found them. However, when he disappeared from me, he disappeared from the whole world. I could not find him online, his phone number or anything. And trust me, as a web designer I knew the ins and outs of the internet to find what we were looking for. My girlfriend and I turned into online stalkers looking for him and a guy that she had once dated, ironically by the same name. This was the beginning of Hottie PI. At one point we found an address where I sent a card saying that I needed some closure, only to have it returned in the mail. In a move I had never done before, I dragged her down to a bar that I knew he used to like only to show up empty-handed. Hottie PI proved to be unsuccessful and I continued back on my road of unanswered questions. At this point I was questioning my own sanity when it came to him.

Months passed and it was time for Lent. To spare my Hottie PI partner's life of more neurotic analysis of Youngeon, I promised to give up talking about him for Lent. Right before Ash Wednesday, I sent a Yahoo messenger contact request to a random series of letters and numbers, thinking strangely that it might have been him. From this point forward, it was time to bite my tongue. I agreed to not talk about him again, and if I felt the urge, I was to start singing Neil Diamond's "Sweet Caroline" instead to take my mind to a happy place.

Through that time, it was business as usual until I got a phone call close to the end of Lent that would take my mind off of the Youngeon completely. "I'm here in Puerto Rico with Josh. He went swimming, was pulled under and is now unconscious, I need you to find his parents." Another friend of mine was in trouble and on his way to the hospital. Everyone in Portland's nightlife scene knew Josh and were waiting on calls about what was going on. As his conditions worsened and worsened, everyone prayed for a miracle. I thought it was a great time for God to show the miracle of bringing someone back, especially on Easter. But it didn't happen. Josh's body gave out on him, and he went to heaven instead on Easter Day.

After the forty days of Lent, my Yahoo messenger chimed as Youngeon sent me a message, but there was no excitement. He initially sent me some message bitching me out about my friend that night in the club long ago, but I told him about my friend's passing and suddenly the energy changed. He was at my house within the hour with a tall hot tea. We lay in my bed all day and he just held me. I think out of complete lack of words to say, he began kissing me again like years ago.

This time, he'd be around a little longer, but something about him seemed so different. That beat-up truck had been traded for a hunk of junk in the driveway. When I asked about the motorcycle he laughed, "Oh, I wrecked that along with about five other ones". When I asked him when the last time he did his great love in life, snowboarding, he said it had been years since doing that as well. He had bounced around from job to job since I had seen him and he was no longer talking with his best friend, and the sister who was his one confidant refused to talk to him. Something was very wrong. It was like he had downgraded on every aspect of his life.

After disappearing one night, part of his standard procedure, he showed up at my house the next day with hickeys all over his neck. At first I was in so much denial that I thought he had got beat up or something. I'm pretty sure I asked him if he had a disease that causes skin rashes. When I realized how stupid that was, I looked him in the eyes and said, "You know that I'm in love with you, correct?" As nice as I could be, I stated that I noticed changes and that he didn't seem like himself. I asked him question after question trying to figure out what was going on with him, when finally he said, "Wow, I feel like I should be on a couch right now, Doctor." Then the therapy session stopped for the day.

The next day, I was working at my computer when the Youngeon drove up to the house for the last time, out of the blue. He had died his hair black overnight. Things seemed very awkward and I just wanted him to get to the point of it all. "I went to my ex-girlfriends last night and begged for her to take me back. She wouldn't take me because I keep coming back to you. I've changed my phone number. I'm never going to talk to you again."

Then he continued to tell me how this girl was not like me, because she was a "bad girl gone bad" and "the kind of girl that he would drive ninety miles per hour across town for just because she needed him." Then his description of his 'love' got bizarre. "She's not intelligent like you or me. She doesn't really care about other people. She is a family girl. She's just so motivated." His tone of admiration of this girl spit out a description of someone I'd never want to have anything to do with and I was shocked this was what he wanted. He told more of their relationship when he stated, "I know you've probably wished that everything I did to you would be done to me, and that's exactly what she has done. But I still love her." At this point, I could only assume he meant the cheating and constantly walking out on me leaving me stranded.

Suddenly I turned into a psychologist again stating that any relationship that pressured him to lose his job, money, friends, family and the things he loved in life was stripping him of who he was. Love this girl or not, she was poison to him and he knew it. Tears welled up in his eyes. I excused myself for one minute upstairs when I heard his car start up. I looked out the window to see him looking back at me crying, and he left my life again. I looked down to what I had grabbed for him in my room. It was a coin with the 4 Way Test from Rotary I had hoped would help to lead his way. It was a coin he'd never get.

That night when I got to the club and ran into his cousin, where the situation began to turn my stomach. He asked how things were with the Youngeon because he knew we were seeing each other again and I said, "He left again. I can't play this person who is constantly around to pick up his life." When he asked what happened, I told him how he went back to the girl he had been dating. His cousin then proclaimed, "He's not dating anyone….. Oh wait, that stripper? I'm sure that's where all the drugs are coming from too." I felt like I was going to puke. All of a sudden everything made sense to me with him and it was unscrambled in my mind:

"She's a bad girl gone bad" = She's a stripper

"She's not intelligent" = She's an idiot

"She's a family girl" = She got knocked up at an early age and is claiming she has to strip to support her child

All of his money was gone = She took it

She was doing the same thing to him as he did to me = She was cheating on him

His strange behavior plus the dramatic weight loss and dead eyes = He had picked up her drug habits

The biggest topper to me was him saying how "motivated" she was in life. At this time, I owned two businesses and was the President of a Rotary club. But, in this guy's eyes, since I wasn't swinging around a pole naked, I lacked motivation.

The final conclusion here was that he and I had so much in common, even down to the exact same relationship problem I had, he chose the Wrong Girls. No matter how well I treated him and how much fun we had together, he still had the impression in his head that love meant being treated like shit. And this time around, that is what he chose.

## Signs You Are Dating a Man Who Choses the "Wrong Girls"

- The person you love can now be seen with trashy women.

- Every area of his life has deteriorated.

- His once energetic personality now resembles something from Night of the Living Dead.

## Final Thoughts on Dating a Man Who Choses the "Wrong Girls"

This has happened to so many of my friends it is disgusting. My friends tend to be intelligent, sexy, driven in respectable job fields, and I'm not going to hide the fact that most of them have looks that stop traffic when they enter a room. There is no hidden reason as to why a lot of my friends are photographed so frequently. All these ladies are successful and prefer to be respected in relationships, but I believe this is where the trouble comes in for this kind of man. Either they believe that they truly don't deserve the "full package", they think abuse is really love, or they don't have as much conscience when disrespecting a disrespectful girl as they would with a girl that deserves to be treated well. No matter what, when someone passes on the positive qualities that you bring to a relationship, sometimes the hardest thing to do is accept that "positive" might not be what this "Wrong Man" is looking for.

# The Junkie

Whether it's cigarettes, alcohol, legal or illegal drugs, I think a majority of the country has tried drugs at one point. Even George W. Bush was arrested for cocaine in the 70's. There are some who have quit, some who use recreationally, and some who even had enough help from daddy to sweep the past under the rug enough to land them in important political positions. Then there are some who let it control their life. Not only does it take them over, but their friends, family, relationships, pets, and work. They become a tornado of disaster in the form of the next Wrong Man.

At a friend's pool party, I met a very hyper man who came on to me so strong. He was pretty cute, so I went out with him a few times. Somehow drug references made their way into every conversation, and he would almost brag about how many drugs he'd done in his life. I'm sure this has worked with girls who did drugs, but having just recently realized that the man I had loved for so many years had turned to a life of hookers and drugs, I had no interest. I brushed it off, but I should have realized that his hyperactivity probably wasn't due to his shining personality.

On another date, we walked along the waterfront and listened to some music. I noticed that a lot of people who knew him would look at this guy in a "what now?" way, very hesitant to stay around long. We bounced around to a few clubs until a local DJ grabbed me and said, "You have to come to Dante's right now. The most legendary DJ you'll ever hear is playing. I guarantee he will blow your mind." He was right, this was the best DJ I had ever heard. But as I was listening to him, I couldn't help but to wonder... where is my date?

I wandered around the club looking for the guy with no luck of finding him. Some time passed and I continued listening to the DJ until I just thought, "OK this is ridiculous!" I walked out the front door and down the street to find my date tweeking out. "Oh my God, there you are!" he said. That's funny, I was right where he left me, at the club we went to together. Apparently, he decided to venture off to find some cocaine down the street and neglected to tell me. I calmly said, "OK. I'm ready to go home," and headed for the car.

At this point in my dating life I was done with the crap. So when he yelled at me down the street "Stop being dramatic!" I calmly turned around and said, "Nope, that's not what I'm doing. I'd just like to go home." We got in the car and headed towards my place. When he asked when we'd see each other again I said, "Well that would be never," he started bawling. Yes, bawling with tears streaming down his face. All I could think is, "You've got to be kidding me." The next phrase out of my mouth would be one that I'd repeat a million times, "Here's the thing" … followed by "You were the one who decided to bail on me to go get coke down the street leaving me, a girl, by myself at a club. You are the reason we won't be seeing each other again." And with that, I was gone.

## Signs You Are Dating a Junkie

- Drugs in their house.

- Sporadic changes in energy levels.

- They'll talk about drugs to gauge whether you accept them or not.

- They have no money.

- They borrow money.

- They steal.

- Similar to a cheater, they lie about where they have been, who they have been with, and what they were doing. You can catch them in the same ways you do a cheater.

- They get irrationally defensive or emotional.

## Final Thoughts on Dating a Junkie

Several of the "Wrong Men" I've dated had used drugs in one way or another. This is another area that social norms have squeezed into acceptance. Some hid the fact, and some were very open about it. The open ones concerned me more because they seemed to think that their drug habit was acceptable. One even would lay pills out on the table when we went out to dinner. Because that's normal?

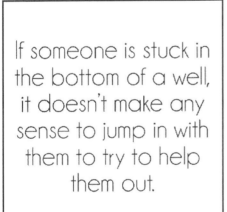

If someone is stuck in the bottom of a well, it doesn't make any sense to jump in with them to try to help them out.

Loving an addict is seeing the person below the addiction. And the difference between this "Wrong Man" and most of the others is that the person they are hurting the most is not you, it's themselves. That person may be the most wonderful, loving thing you've ever come across. But the addiction comes with additions to the relationships that could cost financially, emotionally, and in the worst cases, lives. When dating an addict, you need to weigh the consequences the addiction is bringing to your life. I can't help to think of Lea Michelle's persistence in informing the world of the late Cory Monteith's loving spirit and how he made her feel wonderful every day despite his addiction that eventually killed him. In the case of the Glee sweethearts, it seems as though the positive traits Cory brought to the relationship outweighed his internal struggles. On the other hand, I had a friend whose marriage fell apart because her husband's addiction turned into a life of stealing, lying, layoffs, and endangering their children.

Dating an addict means you accept the fact that you have no control of the other person's addiction. They may quit tomorrow, they may quit two years down the road, or they may be using the last day of their life. Be cautious that your life doesn't become consumed with helping them, but keep a clear eye on the effects the addiction has on your relationship. If someone is stuck in the bottom of a well, it doesn't make any sense to jump in with them to try to help them out. With a realistic and sober perception of your relationship, you can weigh the pros and cons and need to decide if you will accept the addiction or move on.

## **Resources**

Nar-Anon:

> Worldwide fellowships for those affected by someone
> else's addiction.
> nar-anon.org
> 800-477-6291

Al-Anon:

> Strength and hope for friends and families of problem drinkers.
> al-anon.alateen.org
> 888-4AL-ANON

# The Married Man

I think the hardest thing for people to understand about someone's choice in life to try to follow God's path is that the person doesn't automatically don a white robe and vibrant halo over her head turning them into the sin-free pinnacle of ethical perfection like Jesus Christ. One of the entire points of Christianity is that no one is perfect. It might take a long time for God to shape you into who he wants you to be, weeding out the characteristics that reflect a life without him. My point is that everyone makes mistakes, but this "Wrong Man" story is definitely my worst.

The Army Boy came back in town and begged for me to get together with him so he could apologize for the episodes that happened on the Alabama trip so many years ago. Finally, I said "OK" and we met at a restaurant down the street from my house. I coldly sat across from him as he apologized for what had happened. He seemed like he had matured ten years and finally found the words to say to me. He still had that way of telling me that I was the epitome of perfection in his mind when it came to women. I'm not sure why men compare me to food they want to eat, but similar to the Youngeon's apple he told me, "You're just like this chocolate chip cookie that I keep wanting to go back for another bite." After a few hours, and beers, I forgave him.

We sat around drinking on the restaurant patio for hours talking. It felt nice to be around someone so familiar again. I was very lonely in my life and felt hopeless when I thought about relationships. I told him all about Youngeon and how he broke my heart. He told me he had got married and now had a son. Drinking more and more, we walked to another bar to play pool, then we ended up sitting on the top of a hill overlooking a lake. It seemed the more and more time we spent together the more and more he tried to paint his marriage to be a terrible nightmare he couldn't wake up from.

The night carried on and we weren't going our separate ways.

He ended up at my house. We'd say, "OK, You'll sleep in your car" or "OK, you'll sleep on the couch" or "OK, you can sleep on my bed, but with pillows between us" and so on. But it was all bull. Things felt like it was years prior where he had no commitment to a wife or son and it felt so natural to fall into our old ways. We ended up getting together again that night. I had never felt worse about anything I had done. The next morning I wasn't thinking about my selfish self or the Army Boy, but all I could think of was that wife and son.

I told him to tell his wife that I never intended on it happening and let her know I'd never have anything to do with him again. But what he said to her was in his hands from there. Army Boy and his wife went on to have another child. He would try to contact me through the years, but he eventually faded, realizing the cookie shop had closed.

I was a horrible example of what God wanted me to be. My personal slogan for the time was "I'm God's work in progress. If you like what you see, it's because he hooked me up. If not, it's because I screwed it up." I definitely screwed it up this time. I let my personal craving for love and affection get in the way of doing the right thing. This is no excuse. It's the explanation that I had to find about how I got so off course. Even though I took full responsibility for my actions, I let myself down, I let my friends down, but most importantly, I let God down. I never knowingly put myself in a situation where something like that could happen again.

## Signs You Are Dating a Married Man

- That ring on their left ring finger – OR they'll have a tan line from one.

- Much like a cheater, time frames are missing from their day that they can't account for.

- You will always be meeting at your house or a public place.

- If you know about the marriage, they will present the wife as though she is a horrific beast whose evil powers forced them to a wedding chapel and slid a ring of death on their finger.

- They'll use the term "we're separated."

- He accidently introduces you as his wife.

## Final Thoughts on Dating a Married Man

I remember after this happened, I called one of my girlfriends and said, "I really F-ed!" She told me, "I've been on every aspect of that cheating relationship, so I know that you never know what situation you'll find yourself in. You'll just need to forgive yourself at some point and move on." It gave me comfort to realize other people do find themselves in this situation, but it is not an excuse to keep you here. If you haven't picked up one of the major points in this book yet, it's that I don't believe people should get married until that other person meets all the needs they're looking for in life. But once a person has made a commitment before God to another person, no matter how much he loves you, how much he claims he wants you in his life, you must still find that open door to a life of doing the right thing and walk through it.

# The Criminal

If I wasn't born at light speed, I have definitely tried since getting my license at 16 to beat it. I've been mischievous my whole life and have scatters of questionable behavior like sneaking into private property, TPing houses in high school, and rigging vending machines to spit out extra candy. No matter what I've done that teetered on the brink of legalities, I always knew that fine line and have yet to venture across it. The only criminal acts that have been in my life have been left to the

Wrong Men.

At the club one night, I felt like the Cheshire cat was following me around. Everywhere I looked this insanely large smile was peering at me. I'd start laughing and turn away, only to find its owner pop through the crowd at me to make sure I saw him. Almost like Michael Jackson's Smooth Criminal he got me on the dance floor, and it was the most fun I'd had in a long time.

He was this huge goofball and absolute attention whore who probably should have been on an ADHD medication. If he was at an awards show, no matter what name was called, he'd probably say, "Oh, I think they said my name!" and run up the podium. His major problem was that he was always getting into trouble. He'd like to tell people that it was because he was black, but authorities would argue that it was the fact that he was doing wheelies on his motorcycle up the most crowded street in town on a suspended license.

He would blow up my phone like nothing else to get me to go out with him:

"Hello"

"Hi! It's time to play with me."

"Whatcha Doing?"

"You can't ignore me."

"Are you not talking to me because my ass is big?"

This would go on until he got me to respond. I would never recommend this approach to any guy, but somehow he would get me cracking up laughing and eventually, months later, it worked.

My first date with the Criminal was the movies where he was easily the loudest person in not only our theater, but the entire complex. I'm pretty sure the people in the movie next door could hear him. Embarrassed, I crouched down in my seat, but I still couldn't stop giggling at his contagious laughter.

We dated a few months and had a lot of fun together. He reminded me that you can be absolutely silly in life and still be respected. I found a way to laugh again. But one thing landed us in fights constantly. His immature approach to life, which ended him in trouble with the law, constantly contradicted any hint towards a loving relationship. Undoubtedly his greatest example of this while we were dating was when he drove up to the courthouse on a suspended license where the judge literally saw him, then sentenced him to time in jail. There was no passing "Go" and there was no collecting two hundred dollars, he went directly to jail. There were absolutely no conflict resolution skills with this Criminal, and with every disagreement ranged behavior that could reflect every chapter in this book.

Through the next year, we went our separate ways, but it was during this time that we both grew so much because we would keep in touch. Although it was months after we had dated, I got a phone call from the Criminal and surprisingly he figured out something no one else even cared to try. "I get it! You don't have anyone in your life! I mean, where the hell are your parents? You don't have anyone to depend on. I thought you were just nuts, but you're really just constantly preparing for the next person to leave you. Don't worry, I never will!" This was a really cute sentiment, but I had to make sure he understood we were never dating again. However, we remained friends and he always had my back. From time to time, the Criminal would bring back those old days and start a fight by doing something idiotic like harassing a follower of mine on social media. Somehow he'd always find a way to weasel his way back in to my life in front of or behind bars.

The thing was, he was right. I had never dated anyone without the fear that they would just up and be gone. And my history of dating confirmed all those fears. I noticed my psychological cycle that I had with the Criminal where I would try to push him out of my life in order to ease pain in case he did it to me only to turn around to him saying,

"Yep. Nice Try, I'm still here."

He changed too. He would see me dating other people and how I would never settle for someone who was disrespectful or rude. It's like a light bulb clicked in his head when he realized that it might be more beneficial in relationships to be nice to your partner. During one of the last hurrahs with Youngeon, I'd read the Criminal the emails we'd send to each other that were full of respect and love. I remember him saying out of amazement, "People really talk like that?"

He was the last person I expected who would be the one who would put in the time to understand what I am about. Some people come into your life not as a soul mate but as someone to go through it with to learn from each other. I learned not to be quick to judge someone whether they're black, white, hairy, bald, a saint, or a straight up criminal because you never know who will have your back in the end.

## Signs You Are Dating a Criminal

- They're in jail.

- They start ducking down and hiding when driving by cop cars.

- Your new iPhone is missing.

- They tell you, "If anyone asks, I was with you from this time to this time."

## Final Thoughts on Dating a Criminal

You never know what a person is like despite their criminal history, but you can decide if you'd like to date them if they continue with their law-breaking ways. I don't believe in judging people by their past, but if someone continues to break the law time after time bringing you into the mess of it all, it may be time to put this relationship behind bars.

# The Celebrity

Although we're all on the same planet, celebrities live in a different world. For whatever their talent, or lack thereof as many reality stars have found, the public eye changes their human experience, not to mention their approach to their romantic relationships.

My business was extremely popular in Portland and we were involved in all the big events around town. I'd be hired to photograph concerts with recording artists. At a particular event, I never thought the performer was my type, but he ended up being my first date with a guy who had groupies.

He was a Bluegrass artist from Tennessee. I took pictures at his event one night where we met. At the end of the night, several bands and I were relaxing in the green room having a few beers. Soon it was just him and I in the room. I didn't have any interest in the guy until he pulled out his guitar. Looking back, I'm sure this was his "go to" move, but I think this one would have worked on any girl. He started singing a song about how any man who would leave you is an idiot. And that seemed about right to me!

We went out that night and made out a little bit, but mostly we talked. He expressed how he also was trying to follow God and wanted to live his life right. He was amazed that he met a girl who had the same goal, especially at a club event. After hanging out for a while, he headed back east.

We talked occasionally until he came back for another event in a few months. When he did, though, I think he was torn by meeting someone who had potential to settle down with him and his newfound fame.

Everything that night was awkward. There was little conversation and we sat down to watch a movie and he fell asleep. The following day at the show was just the same. After his show, it was obvious that he wanted to go run around with the band and the groupies and didn't want me ruining his fun. So he walked me to my car, and he became that guy from his song who was an idiot for leaving.

I think as cool as it was to find a girl who had the same beliefs, it was still cooler to have fame and groupies. This was the first time I learned that someone who has reached stardom recently is suddenly overwhelmed by dating options and will most likely take them. No matter what, celebrities will have another woman in the next town available, and until they've gotten to the point where they truly want to settle down, they will take their options.

## Signs You Are Dating a Celebrity

- People from every walk of life want their picture with them.

- They have a huge amount of people kissing their ass online or off.

- They have women coming out of woodwork who know details about his every move.

- Women start randomly sneering at you.

## Final Thoughts on Dating a Celebrity

Dating a celebrity can be done. This all takes me back to the amazing, talented, loyal Jon Bon Jovi who married his high school sweetheart and is still married to her to this day. This is undoubtedly one of the facts alone that has put him on the top of my "Top Ten" list of celebrity crushes. One of the sexiest men alive has had women thrown at him since the early 80s and has strong enough willpower to beat off the flock, any man can.

# The Asshole

You may have noticed reoccurring motorcycles in the men I've dated. That's no coincidence; it's my last name. Valentino Rossi is the greatest Motorsport athlete of all time. When a man who owns a bike hears my last name, he freaks out and becomes instantly interested in me. This is what happened with my self-proclaimed asshole.

I was taking pictures one night as this six-foot four New York smartass came up to me and started joking around. He was very attractive, smiled constantly and asked my name. When I said "Rossi" I'm just glad he didn't ejaculate all over the floor. He worked for Ducati, and bikes had been his passion for most of his life. We exchanged numbers and several days later we went on a date.

We met up at a restaurant that had a few pool tables. We got to know each other a bit and I told him that I went to church. "Oh GOD! You're not one of those Bible thumping freaks are you!?" He was so subtle with his words. I explained this was just how things were, and I had no problem with whatever his religion was if he could respect mine.

His complete lack of a filter didn't sway my decision to go out with him again so another night we made plans to go to his house, and I was on my way. His place was about forty-five minutes away from mine. When I was almost there, he called me and said, "Hey, I'm in a bad mood. We shouldn't do this tonight." Irritated that I had already driven across town, I said I was coming over anyway. He was a complete jerk when I got there. He sat and watched TV, not talking to me at all. When I asked what his deal was he stated, "Look, I'm in a bad mood. I told you that on your way over. I'm an asshole. What do you want me to do? At least I'm straight up about it."

I had to respect this guy's honesty. We never dated, but he became one of my best friends. Until he moved, we went everywhere together. Although he claimed to be an "Asshole," it was really more that he was not afraid to speak his mind.

After years of lies and dishonesty from men, this guy was a breath of fresh air. He gave me the courage to follow suit, not beat around the bush in life and state things as they are. It was a quality I rarely found in people up in Portland. So onward and upward in life, I'd go on being a straight shooter, like my friend, but I still choose not to play the role of the "Asshole."

## Signs You Are Dating an Asshole

- They make fun of people they don't know.

- They make rude comments.

- They make fun of people with disabilities.

- They write everything off as "A Joke."

- They put you down.

- They yell at you.

- They say everything is your fault.

## Final Thoughts on Dating an Asshole

Although my Wrong Man in this story was only an "Asshole" according to himself and not a blatant jerk to society, I have seen this horrible trait that some men have eventually destroy some of my friend's relationships with the constant embarrassment and hurt.

I'm going to smack you with a reality check really quick here if you didn't know already. Assholes are probably the weakest humans in existence. They make fun of others in a sick attempt to compensate for their own insecurities. So whether you meet one walking down the street, or you've lived with one your whole life, see them for what they really are but never put up with their treatment if it's directed at you.

# The Player

You're going to run into one. If you don't date one, you're related to one and if you're not related to one, your friend is dating one. They're screwing over your friend, your mom, your sister, co-worker, grocery store clerk, bartender, and daughter. And most likely it's the same player at the same time. The players will come with false promises and quick lines and leave their victims behind. However, no matter how many people he plays, it's always him who stays the loser.

The one good thing about the Junkie who left me at the club so he could buy drugs was that I found a new DJ that I loved listening to. He flew into town every month from Vegas. He was one of the most amazing mash up artists I had ever heard. He still played vinyl records, so watching him was absolutely fascinating. Although his residency was at the Palms Casino in Las Vegas, an irony that came to my life years later, he would come into town every month for a gig. With every month that passed, he would find a way to mix more and more of himself into my life.

> "Are you my birthday present?" he said. I could only imagine how many chicks this guy had said something like that to.

The day we met was his birthday. He was at his monthly gig. A friend of mine and I were out that night and stopped in for some great music. One of the local promoters came up to me and asked me if I had ever met the DJ, and I said, "No." "Well, you've got to meet him! Come on." I was dragged backstage when he was taking a break and we were introduced. "Are you my birthday present?" he said. I could only imagine how many chicks this guy had said something like that to. I may have liked his music, but I could have cared less to be some DJ's groupie. "Nope!" I politely introduced myself and then left.

The next month, I stopped in to see the show. When it was over and I was walking out the door, I heard someone start yelling at me. "HEY! Get back here!" I turned around and the DJ was right behind me. He turned to the promoter and said, "Hey, don't worry about me tonight, I have a ride to the hotel." Apparently, I was that ride.

Completely thrown off by this guy, I said I'd give him a ride. We loaded his crates of records into my Jeep and headed out. I parked the car, and he explained that he could really use some help getting the crates to his room. So I said, "Fine". Everything sounded like line after line. We got to his room, and I just sat on the edge of the bed. He made it pretty clear that most of the time, this is when girls would go spread eagle on him, but I was just ready to leave. Suddenly he says, "You're different aren't you? Are you a believer?" He meant a Christian. I told him I was. At that point he stopped pressuring me and started talking about how he wanted to change his life and settle down soon. He had been DJing since he was fifteen when he toured with MTV and he was nearing forty. It was a great story, but I excused myself and told him it was time to go home. At that point he asked me if I'd come back for breakfast the next day. I gave him my number and said to give me a call.

I never thought I'd hear from that guy again, but my phone rang early in the morning. "Hi, I was serious last night. Let's go to breakfast." So we went to get some food. From there, I ended up taking him to the airport. From the beginning, that's how things were with him. There was always some added benefit to our relationship whether a ride, or a haircut, or a chance to win life-changing prize money.

Again, I figured he would be on that plane and gone, but he called me every day and we'd talk for a long time about life and religion. He would constantly talk about how he had always been a man whore and how he wanted to change his ways. Soon his residency at the Palms was coming to a close, and he wanted to settle down. I knew what he meant because I was getting tired of being out every night for All Club. At the end of every conversation, he always invited me down to Vegas.

It wasn't until another run-in with the Youngeon that I took him up on the offer. Ironically, it was the night before Easter again, and I was out with the Self-Proclaimed Asshole. Youngeon walked straight up to me again and tried to be cute and sweet with me. I just stared blankly back at him. It had gotten to the point where seeing him meant that he was going to leave, and it was going to hurt. I walked away, went over to the Self-Proclaimed Asshole and said, "I think I should go to Vegas." The next day I booked the flight and I was gone the day after that.

I went to one of his Vegas gigs, but it was one of his last. I couldn't help to notice that there was this selfishness about him. He'd start walking through the casino and leave me yards behind him. I just figured, "Screw it. If he wants to walk off, that's fine, I'm in Vegas!" He thought differently. His mind had been so consumed by making music and screwing little groupie girls for so long he had no idea how to treat a person who he actually wanted in his life. We did a few things around town together, and then it was time for me to go home. I was definitely starting to like him, but I knew the distance wasn't anything I was interested in again.

It was also time for him to move to his home town. He packed up all his stuff from Vegas and headed back to his home town halfway across the country. He had made millions in Vegas as a resident, but he had spent millions plus two. He had worked his entire life with nothing to show for it.

Eventually the day came where he called to say, "I'm moving to Portland! A friend of mine is opening a place and I'll be the resident." He was expected to come out for a trial run in a month. We were both pretty excited. I wondered if this was the guy that I was supposed to be with in the end? I mean, things just seemed to be falling into place. We wonder about a lot of things in life, don't we?

The gig he had was one of the coolest I've ever seen. He was paired up with the drummer from White Zombie, and they performed together at a bar outside of town. With each beat, the selfishness got more and more out of control. Then, he started making demands. "Hey, can you bring me lunch? A chicken from the store and some veggies or something? Thanks." Acting as his taxi service and personal take-home delivery girl was getting old quick. The last straw dropped when I was at his club where I saw him smack one of the waitress's asses. We got into the car and got in the biggest fight. We stopped in at Denny's at about 3 am and my eyes just filled up with water. Like many men, this "crying thing" was just too much so he got his stuff from my house.

I was fully prepared to never see him again, but one day he called with some bad news. The club miscalculated on the funding and couldn't have him play anymore. He wanted me to hook him up with a gig at another club while he was in town. When I went to meet up with him, I brought another guy friend and the DJ was livid. The DJ said, "What's it going to take for you to get me a job out here?" Knowing that the industry standard was 10-15%, I quickly said "20%". He glared at me and sneered, "Fine." Unfortunately, this was at a time where every bar in Portland decided that DJs were only worth $250/night, so it wasn't worth much.

We didn't see each other for the rest of the trip.

I think people get lost in the party scene, and this is what he did. All he saw in life were people partying, hooking up, getting crazy, cheating on each other, and women throwing themselves at him. He forgot what people were like outside of the club. He never saw the light of day let alone the light of the fact that there are people out there who are good to each other and someone could possibly be good to him. I didn't want to be in the same place when I was forty, so I knew my days were numbered in nightlife.

## Signs You Are Dating a Player

- They won't make plans down the road.

- They tell you exactly what you want to hear because they've tried every line in existence on every woman who's crossed their path so they know what works.

- You see him getting other girls numbers "for work."

- You run into random girls who seem to know way too many details of your player.

- You find several notches on his bed.

- They call you and every other girl the same pet name.

## Final Thoughts on Dating a Player

I have known several players in my life in addition to the ones I've dated, and there is always one common story that pops up. He caught one girl, usually the first girl he ever dated, in bed with someone else. Then he took it upon himself to screw over every woman he ever met from that point forward. Now we've all heard that two wrongs don't make a right, but neither does one or two wrongs per night from age 18-73. For some reason, men are excused for the emotional thrashing of millions of women around the world while women need to suck it up and move on. As sad as your player's story of his broken heart may be, always keep in mind the thousands of girls' broken hearts that he's caused, and you can probably walk away a lot easier.

# The Revolving Door Ex

I am convinced that immediately after each breakup, every ex in the world somehow activates a "Happiness Radar" which will go on the split second a glimpse of joy appears in your life. Some take the high road of understanding that the breakup was final. Some might return in order to make that long-deserved commitment with you. Then there are the rest, almost in sync with all your other exes, who decide that it is National Ex Day, a day they have determined to further ruin your life.

Compared to the disappearing acts that the Youngeon had done through the years, he was around the clubs quite a bit these days. Usually, he was with one lady or another.

One of the girls was a photographer that I used to employ from time to time. One day she came crying to me when she found out that he had another girlfriend. Yep! That sounded like my Youngeon!

Another time I saw him at a club with an older lady, and he was treating her the same way he used to treat me, like she was the only other person in the room. I heard his cousin say, "It looks like she's been rode hard and hung up wet!" As mean as it was, my jealousy perceived it as funny. I had met her before. The Self-Proclaimed Asshole and I ran into his boss at a club and she was with him. "Oh, that's just some girl that he sleeps with," the Asshole said. Unfortunately, I knew the boss's girlfriend.

For a few months, we emailed each other and something would tell me in my psyche that his message was in my inbox every time. I would be asleep and suddenly wake up at night. I'd look at my phone, and within a few seconds a message from him would show up.

I no longer cared to hold back my frustrations about what he had done, and I verbally puked in every email. I'm pretty sure he thought I had lost my mind, but I didn't care. I had years of emotional steam caused by him and it had to be let out. I eventually calmed down and we were sending loving emails to each other again. I would receive the most beautiful notes from him. He told me that I was a perfect gift from God, and four years after he walked out of my life because I said I loved him, his latest letter finally said he that he loved me too.

We never met up again. An email came one day saying he was in a relationship and needed to stop talking to me. He wanted to marry this girl and start a family. It was the lady the Asshole's boss used to sleep with. I think he found his match in her. I'd never be OK with infidelity, but maybe she didn't mind it. He said she made him happy and brought him back to God. That was the best thing that could happen for him.

One early morning I got in my car after right after midnight. It was the day of his wedding. I started up the car and the radio came on. The song was "Sweet Caroline".

For years, I thought he was "The One". Everything pointed to him, and the fact that he got married made no sense to what I thought was my destiny. I thought having felt that "meant to be" feeling twice was so rare in a lifetime that how could he not be the one? Still, I had learned through the years that truly loving someone meant to love them when they found what made them happy and healthy in life. For him, this wasn't me.

I thought for sure that finding someone with all the qualities from my list on that red piece of paper would be impossible at this point. The only one who came close was gone. Even he never fulfilled my list completely because he constantly treated our relationship like an open-door policy. The red piece of paper was tattered by now and several things had been crossed off even though I thought I had given up. I threw the red piece of paper away, but God didn't. He wasn't done with me. I had a lot of changes coming my way and more tricks up His sleeve than I'd ever expect.

## Signs You Are Dating a Revolving Door

- THEY'RREEE BAAACCKKK!!!

## Final Thoughts on Dating a Revolving Door

Half of the reason I'm writing this book is because I know how it feels to be so devastated by love or the lack thereof in your single life. We all need someone to relate to. We need to know that there is hope. Our hope can lie in whatever we've concocted in our head to be ideal. We hang on and hold tight to the last glimpse of what we think is our happy ending even though it leaves us discouraged, depressed, and rejected when we see our ex's relationship status change on Facebook to "taken." The devastation of giving up hope carries more pain than the loss of any Wrong Man, to the point where we can't see the beauty of another day. That's when encouraging words start to sound like clichés and you start to wonder if the people around you have read one too many Hallmark cards. But this hurt is the same pain you were meant to go through. Only this pain that will show you appreciation of who you are, what you will become, and, most importantly the right man who will have the privilege of walking into your life.

# The Liar

Wouldn't you love to live in a world where you could take everything at face value? Imagine if that amazing car really did come at that "starting at" price without taxes included. Imagine if you could look at the guy across the table from you on a first date and legitimately believe everything he told you about himself without your head screaming "This is a crock!" We're forced to wander through our lives, day by day, making assumptions about people's honesty, only wishing for the mystical polygraph tests of a person's nose growing or pants catching on fire.

I was hired for an event that was going to change my life. It was going to be streamed online live and I was going to be the host.

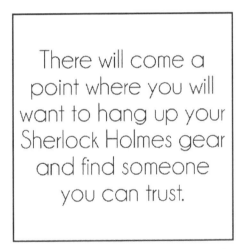

However, when the event organizer booked me, he said, "I need a DJ. I need the best in the world and I need someone with a name." Only one person came to mind. I gave him the Vegas DJs number.

Soon I got a call from him. "Hey, I have an event I'm doing out in Portland!" "Yes, that would be the event I got you," I said. Again, he benefits. He said he wanted to see me when he was here, and he was upset at how things were left. The months working up to the event, we talked on the phone and Skype all the time. He would tell me how much he cared about me and really thought we should try to see if we were going to go somewhere this time around.

He landed in town a week or so before the gig and we were doing great. He picked up a few common decency habits that were nice, like walking next to me in public. Plus, we had already had a huge blow up and he came back, so I wasn't afraid of him leaving again. The plan was to do the event and then head to the beach a few days later.

The day of the event came and chaos ensued. It almost felt like we were an old married couple when I heard a voice on the mic, "Janice Rossi, there are M&Ms in this trail mix you brought me and I cannot eat M&Ms." That was my trail mix and apparently he had adopted it. As bad of a reference to the mistress in Good Fellas Janice Rossi was, I couldn't help to think it was adorable. We were running around the venue getting our stuff in line to pull it off. He was relaxing in my dressing room when one of my best girl friends came in to do my hair. After I was done, he said he needed some help with his own hair so she started working on it. That's when I was called in to start working.

It was one of the best nights of my life. I absolutely loved the camera and wanted to find a way to host events like this all the time. The producer came up to me yelling, "You're doing awesome! Everyone online just wants you to come back on, and we're pulling some of the other hosts!" Nothing could get better. I got glowing reviews and was so proud. The event closed down and everyone left. Suddenly, on the mic I heard, "Janice Rossi, please come down to the stage." I headed to where the he was, he put his hand on the floor and spun around a million times doing a windmill. Technically, he was not supposed to be doing this because he had had hip replacement surgery because of break dancing injuries, but he knew I had never seen him do it, so he put on a show. We were so exhausted that night we both passed out.

The next day he told me that he had set it up with my friend to get his haircut. I dropped him off at her salon and went on my merry way.

The day after that, we headed for the beach. He was in his own world, blankly staring at things around him and barely talking. When I started putting the moves on him, he told me, "I can't just have sex all the time!" We hadn't had sex in a while. I hadn't had sex in a while. It would be a long time until I found out what he meant by that statement.

He left town and I didn't hear from him again. I'd call through the months with no answer. Even on his birthday there was no response. I'd be sitting in the car with one of our mutual friends who was on the phone with him, but he would not talk to me.

Sometimes in life, you will not have the answers when you want them and people will lie directly to your face. Sometimes you'll never get them and need to find a way to move on. But sometimes, down the road, the truth will come out and everything will start to make sense.

## Signs You Are Dating a Liar

- Just let them talk. None of their stories add up.

- They cover their mouth or nose while talking.

- They can't look you in the eye.

- They get defensive at general questions.

- They're fidgety.

- They will over-exaggerate details in a story.

- They repeat sentences not only trying to convince you of their lies but themselves as well.

## Final Thoughts on Dating a Liar

Call it women's intuition, psychic abilities or the fact that you have been lied to so many times in life, there comes a point where the whole practice of being a private investigator becomes second nature. As much as some men want you to brush their lies under the rug, there is a huge difference between some lies and telling people the wrong age or weight. Being with a liar for too long is exhausting and there will come a point where you will want to hang up your Sherlock Holmes gear and find someone you can trust.

# The Client's Relative

As a single person you'll hear, "You're never going to meet your soul mate at a bar. You're never going to meet them at a concert." This list will go on to casino, laundry room, school, frat party, public bathroom, church, online, pretty much anywhere humans interact with other people. So you'll think, "OK, I'll meet them through someone I know." You know what? You could meet the person of your dreams at any random location, at any time, through any person, but you can also meet the ones you wish you never met.

I had several clubs in town that I was working for and one in particular was very accommodating to me. When I would arrive, they would shower me with plates of food for me and all my friends. After hours, they would load up the Hookah pipe and we'd stay until four in the morning. They felt like family to everyone. But in my case, I think they wanted to solidify the deal.

My client's nephew was attractive and helped out at the bar once a week. His uncle was determined to get us together and was always reintroducing me to him. We'd all hang out in groups eating large meals after the club was closed. Then one night, my client decided to trick me into it being a date. He set up a table in the back room with candles on it. Conveniently, no one else could stay for dinner but his nephew. Laughing at the "set up" the entire time, the nephew and I sat down to eat. About a half hour though the meal, the hairdresser friend of mine came prancing in drunk out of her mind. She pulled up a seat with us and started eating off of our plates. Apparently her drunkenness was more important than the fact that we were obviously on a psudo-date.

It became very awkward with the three of us and eventually she asked if he could show her to the bathroom. They never came back. I went into the other room and sat down with a few people for about a half hour, then got up to leave. I couldn't find the two anywhere, so I went home.

Several days later, the nephew called me and asked me on a date. When I asked him what had happened that night, he claimed that he showed her the bathroom and took a call outside so I agreed to the date and we went out to dinner the following week. He was very polite and we had a few things in common, but he was extremely aggressive with me physically. At one point, I walked out of the bathroom to find him standing there, where he started making out with me. Part of me thought it was exciting, while another part felt it was creepy. We went our separate ways that night and I had a strange feeling.

The next day was Valentine's Day, and I called the friend who had disappeared with him that night. "Oh yeah, I have been meaning to call you about that." According to her, he followed her into the bathroom, took his pants off and forced her into giving him a blow job. From the way he was acting on our date, I completely believed it! I texted him that day and said, "Lose my number." Even though he kept asking questions, I never talked to him again.

## Signs You're Dating a Client's Relative

- A crooked "Match Maker" look in your client's eyes!

## Final Thoughts on Dating a Client's Relative

I think you're taking as big of a chance dating a client or relative of a client as you would dating your best friend. Ideally, this person could be wonderful. You know he has some finances behind him and family support. But if things go wrong it could leave your client and your relationship in a very awkward place regardless of who was in the bathroom making out with your friend. In the end of every client/relationship situation, blood is stronger than a cash register and you could lose a client in the end.

# The Right Boss

The economy in Portland was tanking. In three years, twelve of the clubs I did business with closed. My business took a 75% decrease and something had to be done. I threw an insanely successful event that should have brought in money to tide things over, but even the sponsors were spreading out the money they owed me over several months in breach of our contracts. I prayed to God for a miracle, and I was about to receive the greatest in my life.

Several years prior, I had met a videographer at a wedding. He stated that his buddies were taking some of their work to networks, but he was really interested in filming more of the club events around town. He was married, so everything was very professional. I took his information and told him I'd call him if something came up.

About a year after that, I ran into him at one of the clubs with his friend. His friend was hitting on me HARD. It turned out, they got the TV show and he was in the process of a divorce. From that point forward, we started talking all the time. He became my new best male friend and we could talk about anything. Every problem I had with men, which would heighten my insecurity, he would build me up and make me feel like a rock star. We were there for each other in life and in business. Through it all, we had the same beliefs and faith in God.

At the same time, I was growing tired of many things in Portland. I was done with the rain, the men, and, especially of losing money in the great northwest. After talking to my new videographer friend, I decided to move down to where he lived in Las Vegas. However, I needed a job.

After looking at a few resources online, I stumbled upon the name of someone who was my business idol when I lived in California. Through all of my business courses, two brothers in town were the image of success. The brothers not only owned the Sacramento Kings, but they had built one of the most famous, celebrity-packed casinos of all time in Las Vegas, The Palms. They were hiring a web designer for their skateboarding event, and the job listing required the exact same thing I had already done in Portland with All Club. I emailed immediately:

*"To Whom it May Concern,*
*I saw your job listing for a web designer, and I am your candidate. I've developed websites for over ten years and I have had extreme success building the kind of site that is exactly what you are looking for. That and the fact that I can tell any Blazer fan that the Kings are better."*

At eleven PM that night, I got a phone call from one of the men in charge. He asked me to go over their current website and send a proposal as to what I would do with it. The next day by two PM it was done, in complete detail. The day after that, I was offered the job. The only catch was that I needed to move to Vegas by that following Tuesday to meet with the infamous brothers.

I had to tell my clients what was going on, so I met with each of them to break the news and set them up with new contacts. There was one client of mine that was a business owned by some siblings. Through the years they had acted very inappropriate with me, grabbing my ass and making sexual comments at every turn. I very easily could have had a sexual harassment suit with this company, but I never took that opportunity, as often as it came. Every dime they owed me was a fight to get out of them as I'd watch them turn around with a wad of cash on their way to the strip club. Through the years, I had brought them millions in sales from members on my website, but they would insult me making statements suggesting they should just pay me in Taco Bell coupons. The time came to tell them what was going on, and nothing felt better than this day.

"I am going to be having Chris here come in and work with you because I will be moving to Las Vegas. I was hired by another set of brothers."

"Oh yeah?" one said. "Who's that?" not even looking away from the food he was eating.

I told them who had hired me.

Silence.

They didn't say another word. I wished them the best of luck and I was on my way.

That was the fastest move in history. I drove straight with my Jeep attached to the back of the UHaul and a nervous 100-pound Malamute in the cab. I was off to sun, and nothing could turn me back.

The day came when I met one of the brothers. Our first meeting was filled with my excitement plus my determination to fix the horrible disaster they had going on with their current website. I had to keep telling myself to not act like a star-struck girl. When I met the first brother, it was instantly clear we were going to work greatly together. At a board meeting, after overcoming the fact that I was at a board meeting with one of the famous brothers from my marketing classes, I hung on to every word. I could see why he was known to be one of the amazing marketers in the world. He wasn't just smart, he was giving and fair. He wanted to give the customers what they were looking for, even if it meant providing solutions for an entire industry, including his competitors. The bigger picture he saw was held together by the ingrained morals of his family.

I wasn't technically supposed to be working for another few weeks as they were in the process of letting go of the previous web developers, but I didn't have anything else to do so I redesigned the site on another server. Four days away from our big competition, one of the brothers asked me to meet them at the Palms the next morning. I headed down to hear his frustration and embarrassment about putting on this event with a non-functioning website that looked like crap. He said, "If you would change it, what would you do?" "I've already done what I would do," I said. He was confused, so I showed him what I had been working on. Since my laptop decided to crap out on me, I jumped on one of the Palms administrative computers. His eyes lit up. "YES! Finally, a professional!" He started making phone calls. "Why is it that we have been paying this other company a fortune to do nothing and this girl comes in here in a few days and fixes everything!?"

"Little Lady, you need a new computer!" And he handed me something that made me freeze in my tracks, his black credit card and his ID. He hooked me up with a driver, and I was on my way. I nervously walked around Best Buy clenching the cards to my chest and occasionally calling my father, asking him details about the latest computers on the market. I went to the counter with my decision and told them I had my boss's card with me. "We can't take a card if it's not yours." Then I laid down the ID and the clerks said "Is this your boss?" "Yes," I said and called the driver who was wearing a Palms polo. "OK, I guess we can make an exception." New laptop in hand, and working for the Right Boss, I was ready to take on Vegas.

# The Wrong Friend

Whether you're single or in a relationship, girlfriends are the best things ever. Someone in your life who knows all your stories, knows exactly what "That Look" on your face means, is there with a shoulder to cry on and a cocktail for any occasion. Though my friendships have come and gone through the years, depending on relationship status, physical location or the natural changes in life, my friendships became a stable support of the person I was to eventually become. However, here and there, sprinkled in with the glitter that is the group of my girlfriends, would appear a wolf in designer, yet purchased at an amazingly discounted price, clothing.

Almost a year later, I got a call from the DJ telling me why he had disappeared on me. Back when I had dropped him off to get his hair cut by my supposed good friend, the trim took a detour. Apparently, they went to a local hotel and got a room. I guess I should have realized that haircuts don't take an entire day. He had tried to pawn off the chore of telling me on my friend, but she never did. The comment about him not being able to have sex all the time made sense finally!

I was disgusted that my supposed friend held my hand as I cried about this guy. I will never understand how she could continue to fake a friendship with me, doing everything together including going to church. Suddenly the story she had about her near-rape experience with my client's nephew shed a new light as well.

> Sprinkled in with the glitter that is the group of my girlfriends, would appear a wolf in designer clothing.

Most people in this world are decent people, and most can be relatively good friends or at least respectful acquaintances. But if you have any hint of success in life, you have the potential of meeting someone with such insane jealousy to the point where they will do horrible things. A lot of times, the person will be so manipulating that you won't see it coming. However, I have a theory that it takes two years to really figure out what a person is all about and the disgusting behavior will definitely reveal itself in this time. It certainly did with me. Right along with all the wrong men in this book, she was dumped.

## Signs You Have a Wrong Friend

- You find her copying your behavior, clothes, and activities.

- She actively pursues your loved one interest online.

- Suddenly movies like Single White Female make all too much sense.

- She throws herself on your love in public.

- She insists on being in situations that leave her alone with your significant other.

## Final Thoughts on the Wrong Friend

As in relationships, friendships can have their ups and downs and most situations are salvageable with some apologies and work on everyone's part to move forward. Sometimes you can get just as hurt by a friend leaving your life as you can a "Wrong Man". When a girl is fueled by rage and jealousy to the point where her path of destruction has no off switch, it's better to realize that she was no friend at all.

# The Man Still In Love With His Ex

So often, when we look at our dating pasts, we shake our heads and think, "Oh dear God, never let me meet someone like that again!" Even when we truly had a deep love that is lost, something inside us says that there is something better out there. At the very least, it says to show the person that you choose to date in the future some respect and don't let him ever get it in his head that someone else is even close to the importance he is. For whatever reason, these natural signs of courtesy are completely disregarded by some people in the dating world and you're left feeling as though you're on the side lines in a relationship long gone.

Years prior in Portland, the Professional Bull Riders were in town and I was the furthest thing from a cowgirl. However, I was hired to take pictures at an autograph signing at the country bar with one of the bull riding teams. While I was there, one of those riders kept smirking at me. All these girls would be in line to take a picture with him and he eventually gave one of them my camera so she could take a picture of us together. I had no idea where this was going, I just hoped it didn't result in being in a pasture tipping cows.

When the night ended, I was on my way out. I guarantee I did not have a sign on me that said TAXI, but again, this guy assumed I would be taking him home. We were out in the parking lot and he told his limo driver, "Hey, I'm just going to go with her." He didn't want to go home yet, and I had mentioned that I was going to a few other places that night so he thought he'd tag along.

I have never gotten more crap from people at the clubs than that night when I brought this trouble maker in tight pants, belt buckle the size of a Frisbee, and a big-rimmed hat. I also had never had more girls throw themselves at someone I was hanging out with before. He was happy-go-lucky everywhere we went. If I showed him something new, like shrimp chips, he'd be as ecstatic as a little kid.

All the way back to his hotel, he would crack jokes and yell like the cowboy that he was from my Jeep with the top down. Once we got to the hotel, he came in to kiss me. He got away with a little one, but I said goodnight and was on my way. We exchanged numbers and I would hear from him from time to time, but I wouldn't see him again for years.

•     •     •

He lived on his own ranch where there wasn't much phone service and he would literally be out herding animals most of the time, but occasionally through the years, the PBR Cowboy would call or text me. The closest I'd ever got to that lifestyle was watching *Little House on the Prairie* as a child. Since Las Vegas is one of the main stops for the National Finals Rodeo, I decided to get in the ring.

This cowboy was always saying, "I'm just looking for that little lady to come back to my farm with me, and you've always caught my eye." As un-attractive of an offer as that was for me, a girl who freaks out if her internet strength is not at full bars, it was cute to hear. He was jam-packed with activities all over the strip and dragged me along. I'm pretty sure he thought he was on a horse that night, yelling at all the drunk people on the street and joking, "I need to know where the Swingers Club is!" One thing was for sure, he would not stop with the come-ons! We'd be riding in a packed taxi and, even though he chose to ride in the luggage area to be funny, I'd feel his hand coming around the seat constantly, trying to tickle me. Time after time, he kept trying to kiss me and I kept turning away seeing the hopelessness of this becoming anything long term. Finally, after he swung me around the country dance club's floor a few times, a girl said, "Kiss him already!" so I did.

I'm not sure if he confused me with a bull from his line of work, but he was aggressive as all hell! I came home to find out he had given me something I hadn't even thought about since high school. A hickey! As entirely too old that we were, it brought up that old competitive reaction - "Game On, Cowboy!" Now keep in mind, he set the bar as to what was acceptable here. The next day after messing around a bit, he went to the bathroom. "DAMMIT WOMAN! What in the hell is this!" He came walking out with a dark hickey on his neck. Opps! Looks like he got some payback.

Now, I work from home so if something like this happens to me it's not that big of a deal. However, since he was injured, he was hired to commentate on the event on national TV that weekend and he had strict requirements about his appearance from his sponsors. That was one of the quietest car rides I had ever been in, sprinkled with statements like, "They better have good makeup artists". I never heard from him again on that trip and I felt terrible.

Two weeks passed and I gave him a call saying that I wanted everything to be cool between us and we talked. What unraveled in our conversation was that I wasn't the only bull in his ring. Apparently he was still married to a woman who had left him and lived in the states with two of his kids. I'm still not sure how taking me to live on his farm with him would have worked into that equation. When I asked him what his plans were with his ex, the stubborn cowboy stated, "Well I'm not going to divorce her! I made a promise, and she can run off all she wants, but I'm not giving her a divorce!"

I've been down this road before, and it had been bad enough when a guy I had been with had no legal or parenting ties to some girl from his past. My bull rider days came to a close. While dealing with men who are so determined to hang on to something, it's better to walk away knowing he's more full of bull than he is working with one.

## Signs You're Dating Someone Still In Love with Their Ex

- They're frequently brought up in conversations.

- They try to invite them to events.

- They always compare you to them.

- They tell you they are still "friends" with their ex.

## Final Thoughts Dating Someone Still In Love with Their Ex

Maybe they don't like change. Maybe they don't want to admit defeat. Maybe they have so much regret over one situation or one person that they screwed over that they cannot get this person out of their mind. So they dedicate their life to a person who no longer cares to give them a chance. Having dated the "Man Who's Still In Love With His Ex" so many times in my relationships, I talked to my counselor about the situation and she told me this story.

There was a couple she had seen in her past who came in having marital problems. They were miserable. The wife was constantly inviting her ex-husband to holiday dinners, events, even just casually over for dinners. Through the wife's manipulating presentation of the situation, the husband felt he couldn't say anything about how he felt about having her ex in his life. After many sessions with the counselor, the man finally let it out, "Why IS this guy at our house all the time? I didn't agree to this!" The counselor stated the obvious to the wife, "You're trying to have two husbands." Then the counselor turned to the husband and said, "This is not fair to you. You need to decide if you want to put up with this anymore."

Needing a little more convincing since so many exes had tried to rationalize their exes in my life, I decided to do a survey on my website. I polled about fifty people, twenty-five men and twenty-five women, on what I called "The Ex Factor." The results were fascinating. In short, I found two things:

1) The majority of people thought it was fine to maintain a friendship with their ex while they are in a relationship.
2) The majority of people did not want the person they were dating to maintain a friendships with their exes while they were together.

That right there tells me how selfish wanting to keep an ex around in your life is when you're in a relationship.

This validated my feelings on the subject and made it clear to me that even if you're being told you're the most important person in a relationship, if the person you're dating will not get rid of his ex, the only two people that are important in that situation are the ones who arrived first. It's fine to have respect for an ex and be nice at social functions, but having them in your life on a daily basis while you're dating someone else is pure selfishness. Everyone has exes, and there are plenty of people out there who will leave their exes where they belong, in the past.

# The User

There is a time in life when you realize you have a lot to offer. It could be right out of the womb, or it could be many years later, after having to overcome the fact that everyone around you has tried to tell you otherwise. But that day will come. And almost as quickly as it comes, people will be there to try to take advantage of everything you have that is of any benefit to them. Some of them might even be the Wrong Men you date.

It's amazing the points made in the movie When Harry Met Sally that we refuse to believe. A distant friendship between a guy and a girl is exactly that, a friendship. If a friendship develops into a relationship in which he is the first person you see in the morning and the last person you see at night, something's inadvertently to happen. This person knows everything that has happened with everyone you've dated and gave you the right solution to every time someone broke your heart. You have your own secret world, where only you two make sense and the rest are paranormal. Nothing like this can last long without both people questioning what would happen if you take it to the next level.

Through the course of several years, a relationship with one guy friend and I got to the point where we become inseparable. When I lived in Oregon, he was my "Go To" guy for everything and I was his "Go To" girl. When I moved to Vegas, we spent nearly every second together. We'd grab our computers and go to each other's houses just to be around each other even though we were both busy with what we had to get done. We even had projects together where I started managing his bookings and his website. So the day came where we both were questioning if there was more there, when it all came out on the table. For weeks we teetered, knowing we were each interested in taking it somewhere else. Inevitably, our friendship took a turn into uncharted waters never to return. Finally, after a promotional event for his work, he kissed me. The kiss that would destroy our friendship.

Years ago, I had tried dating my best guy friend and it went well despite the long distance. This time around, I would learn that even though so many people use the phrase "the best relationships start out as friends," the worst relationships can also start out that way. This new guy friend was becoming famous with his new TV show. As I stated with the musician I had spent some time with, the excitement of women throwing themselves at you is an ego boost that takes a while for celebrities to outgrow of, if they ever do. My friend was right at the beginning of becoming famous and was sucked into the attention from these women, but still wanted to attempt a relationship with me. There was no way this approach would work with who I was. When we decided to date, I figured he knew everything about the jerks I had dated, so there was no way he'd act like one of them. However, every "You shouldn't put up with…" statement he ever said to me was exactly what he wanted me to put up with, with him. At one point, we planned a trip together to Disneyland. It was a few days later that one of his groupie girls told me that he had invited her along. Going places together turned from being side by side to him ditching me as soon as possible to make it look like he was "available" to his fans.

> There are even people who calculate what's in it for them when they see that "share" button on Facebook.

All this was minor in comparison to who he was becoming. His job and his fame made him someone who I probably never would have been friends to begin with. It all snuck up on me so fast. I can imagine it's how you'd feel when your own child has grown two inches but you don't see it because you're with him or her every day. One of our first conversations was about our faith in God, but through our years of friendship, mine had grown stronger and his had dissipated. Our talks that used to be filled with both of our interests started solely becoming about his. All the things he used to say to build me up as a person and friend were replaced by statements of how I didn't really matter. We went from having two different dreams in life and helping each other achieve them to having one. That one was his. Prior requests to "Hang Out" were replaced with "Can you do this for my business?" "Can you build/manage my website?" "Can you organize this order?" I was getting assumptions that I would bail on my paying job with a highly respected family to attend to his every demand! He was no longer my close friend. He had become another Wrong Man I was dating.

We ended it as soon as it began. This quickly became one of my most devastating experiences with a Wrong Man and I couldn't handle the fact that this man who really knew me had no qualms about hurting me. My respect for him was gone, along with our friendship. Knowing how I am about making a clean break from men, he went for the worst possible approach to salvage anything with us. "I'm going to kill myself if you aren't my friend! I'll do it! I'll post it all over the internet saying you're the reason I did this." That's where panic set in. I called every suicide line in existence. The lines said to contact people close to him for more help and those people said "Oh, he says that all the time. He won't do it." Out of ideas and completely freaked out, I went to a counselor. She said, "Well, he definitely played the trump card on you with a suicide threat. I mean, there's not much more you can do with that." She continued to state that his suicide threats were a sick, controlling maneuver to get what he wanted from me. The best solution would be to never have anything to do with him again. So I followed her advice.

Years later, he's still alive. At one point one of his fans told me that he tried to publicly announce to his fans that I had hacked his website in what was a very clear attempt on defamation of character on his part. In reality, he just never paid the bill. I had missed all of this because I took a different approach than his fans when I no longer paid him any attention.

Taking that step from friendship to relationship is one not to be taken lightly. My recommendation is to always remember how you've seen them act in other relationships as a sign to how they might treat you. Things probably won't change when you're the girl in the passenger seat just because you started as his friend. I've had a 50/50 result of the experience being positive, but in both cases I lost my best friends when it was over.

## Signs You're Dating a User

- Every conversation is about them.

- Everything you do benefits them in one way or another.

- They will expect you to do things for free that you normally would get paid a lot of money to do.

- They keep trying to get and use your contacts.

## Final Thoughts Dating a User

One common trait that you see in a person who is constantly getting taken advantage of in relationships and friendships is their ability to give. From an early age, we're taught in school to share. So it's no surprise that the good people in the world think the right thing to do is to share with others. But for every good person, there's someone out there who only wants to take. Maybe they missed that day in kindergarten. Maybe they can't put together why people are always irritated when they call. There are even people who calculate what's in it for them when they see that "share" button on Facebook. Relationships have to be a give-give situation, because if one person gives all they've got without receiving anything, they'll just be left standing there empty-handed in the end.

# The Drunken Idiot

Eventually, I tried online dating one last time. I didn't know a lot of people in Vegas, so it was a great way to meet new people. However, I definitely noticed a difference from the men in Vegas to the ones in Portland. Every man I went on a date with would say, "Wow, you're the first girl that hasn't asked how much money I make." What is totally inappropriate for women to do in any other city in the world had apparently become standard in the Vegas dating scene. That, or the ratio of hookers to datable women was way off. I'd also get hit up on a regular basis on the site by men who wanted a "date" with me while they were in town for a visit. I'm thinking they really were looking for a hooker but didn't want to pay for it.

However, I started talking to one guy who was from Portland. It had turned out that we had a lot of the same friends and he was in Vegas quite a bit for business. Our mutual friends were really good people, so I based quality control on the fact that I didn't think this group would hang out with a shithead. We planned on going on a date the next time he was in town, another decision I would come to regret.

The Palms at the time had a comedy tour that came through every Wednesday night that I would go to pretty frequently, so the plan was to have dinner at the Palms and go to that. After meeting him at one of the bars, we headed on our way. We sat down to dinner and within several minutes I couldn't help but wonder if I was the girl on the date or the waitress was. Whenever she walked by he would holler at her and start flirting with her for an uncomfortably long time. I sat there turning my head in any other direction, as if that could avoid how completely wrong this was. During his date with the waitress, I texted one of our mutual friends asking about this guy, but got no answer. As if to break the awkwardness, bread finally came to the table. Of course awkwardness turned to disgust as he went through the basket touching every last piece with his grubby hands. When he finally chose one, he started double dipping in the butter dish then shoving what looked like tablespoons of butter on the end of his bread into his mouth. It made me never want to use butter on food again. I decided I didn't want any bread anyway.

Occasionally he'd strike up a conversation. Usually it was about himself. At one point, however, he did ask me something about myself. In mid-sentence he picked up his phone, called his friend and started talking to him. The only conversation that really involved me was when he found out my friend worked at the golf course and he wanted a hookup. I don't normally mind splitting the bill with guys on dates, but this one I had absolutely no problem pushing him the check. On the way to the comedy club he disclosed that he was on pain killers. Apparently, his own personality wasn't enough to ruin an otherwise good night, so he had to add drugs. The entire time at the club, he tried to get me to drink more. Although getting hammered would have been a lot more fun than being with him, I could tell he was just trying to get me drunk to take advantage of me so I passed. When I would say, "No, I'm good," he would start calling me a "pussy". Because THAT is how you get a girl to like you! At the end of the show, he wanted to meet the comedian and I gladly parted ways with him. I went to the back of the room where the opening act was. It turned out that the opening act was the coordinator of the event and he also worked with the brothers I was working for. We were in conversation when the drugged-up bad date came back. The opening act asked me, "How did you start working for them?" which started the dialog that would seal the deal for worst date in my entire life.

Idiot Date: "She gave the brothers a blow job!"

Me: "Nope. Not at all"

Opening Act: "Um… is this your boyfriend?"

Me: "No. Not by any means"

Idiot Date: "Yeah, we're just going to go up to my room and have sex."

Me: "Actually, the more you talk, the less likely I will ever have anything to do with you for the rest of my life."

And the night was over with him asking, "Wait, can I still get that deal at the golf course tomorrow?" I told him to call my friend. First, I made sure that she worked on commission and told her to mark his cost up 200%.

I got hold of our mutual friend the next day. "That guy is an asshole! We used to be really good friends, but he borrowed my car one night, destroyed it and never paid me for it!"
Note to self: Call the mutual friends first.

## Signs You're Dating a Drunken Idiot

- Swerving while walking or on the road.

- Unnecessary loud talking.

- They're the only ones embarrassingly laughing at their own jokes.

- Picking fights with random strangers.

- He's smacking the waitress's ass.

# Pinpointing Your Value

Everyone has value, but I don't think many can actually put a dollar amount to it. I wouldn't call it "lucky" that I had a situation where I could put a value on myself, but it does make for an interesting story.

Despite the fact that the DJ slept with my friend when we were together, I had to respect his coming clean to me. I think out of my straight loneliness of losing another best friend, we talked on the phone a lot through the next year, and I even stopped by his town to see him while traveling. We were supportive of each other's endeavors, but I had no idea that my next decision would bank him so much.

I lived in Vegas and was constantly hearing what the DJs in town were doing. Since he was so respected by them all, they would constantly ask me about him and tell me to relay what they were up to. However, since he left the Palms, the promoters wouldn't be calling him anymore. I remember I told one of my close girlfriends who hired acts to look at him, but she said she couldn't sell him. Down the road, it came to my attention that there was a TV show auditioning DJs to film a reality contest where DJs went head to head with each other week in and week out until there was only one man standing. The DJs I knew in Portland, LA, and Vegas were all trying out for it. The one I had dated living in Podunk, Nowhere, hadn't even heard of it yet.

Auditions were getting closed up and there were only a few cities left that they were stopping into, so I called my old fling. "This is yours. You need to do this contest," I said. He went into some rant and rave, as he always did, about how they're all a setup, they're all a conspiracy, etc. Then, it came out that he really had no money. So I got online. I paid an insanely high price for a next-day ticket to the Atlanta audition. Conspiracy and all, he went, and I got the call immediately following. They gave him a standing ovation at the tryout. And he was on his way.

The recording of the show was all in secret but every week or so, I'd still get a phone call.

"You won't believe it! So and so is gone, so and so is gone, and I'm still in it!"

"Holy shit, I'm down to the last five."

"It's only me and two other guys, and I'm only worrying about one of them."

The filming was over and he was more ecstatic than ever. "I want to come out and see you! I want to marry you, you have no idea. I can't tell you what happened, but I'll tell you that no matter what, I got the exposure I needed to save my career!"

Although I had never been wise in dating, my business sense told me that dating me really was starting to look like a good investment.

Our magic by this time had worn off completely, but I'm always interested to see if people change for the better, so I told him to come out. He spent about a day of being lovey, and resorted back to his bad behavior of forgetting I was in the same room as him, having me taxi him around town and bailing on me with his friends. On the day he was flying home, I was flying up to Portland so I told him, "At the very least, can you make sure you pick me up on the way to the airport? I need to be there at the same time that you need to be there, at three AM." At 2:30, I get a phone call. "Hey, we're not going to make it, you're going to have to find your own ride. Also can you bring the bag I left at your house?" I had to pay $60 for a cab and was almost late for my flight. I dropped his bag off at his feet and that was the last I saw of him until the show came on TV.

I never watched the episodes, but I knew where it was going. I'd see the hype on social media, and that same girl promoter friend of mine came back at me asking me for his number about halfway through. Then the day came where she told me he won the whole thing. Even though this guy did one of the worst things anyone has ever done to me while dating, I don't regret helping him out. He took responsibility for his actions, and that's the best someone can do once the damage is done. That didn't mean I'd date him again, but I could put my value at least $250,000, additional prizes, and a saved career. Although I had never been wise in dating, my business sense told me that dating me really was starting to look like a good investment.

# A Man with a Secret

I have a theory that within the first three months of dating someone, you're going to see the best of the best even if it meant seeing some little white lies. Whether it's a lie about how much money they make complete with knock-off Rolex, the fact that they live with their parents or that toupee on their head, there is no worse secret to find out about your new date than the ring they're hiding in their pocket.

While out and about with that same girl promoter friend of mine, we ran into a group of the guys from Nellis Air Force Base. One of the guys in the group stood out from the rest. Initially I'd think it was the fact that he was six four, but it was probably more that he kept doing things to try to get my attention. I think the whole first night was innocent flirting until something happened that brought a reality check into the evening. Of course, it wasn't until the end when I found out the severity of our entire time together.

While going through counseling after my marriage, I did therapy sessions that were developed for the military for Post-Traumatic Stress Disorder because the therapist thought that the trauma in my childhood and past relationships were the underlying issues to my insomnia. However, this came in handy when out with this military man. At one of the bars, my friend said something and he got up, angrily dropped his glass, and was about to explode. Something just kicked in and I grabbed him, looked him in the eyes and said "Hey, we're ok here. You're fine." And he settled down. He told me no one has ever been able to break him out of that before. That started a connection that should not have happened.

We spent the time before he left doing fun things around town and overdosing on Jon LaJoie sketches on YouTube. Every day became filled with back and forth flirting jumping from email to Twitter. It really felt like we were falling for each other and eventually we told each other that. At a play one night we sat in the most perfect seats in the house, but all I could see out of the corner of my eye was that he was sneaking peeks at me, not observing what was happening on the stage. But the day came when he left. I felt it was very strange that his "Goodbyes" were so permanent, when I thought such a great beginning deserves a follow up. He only lived an hour flight away, so why was this farewell forever?

When he left, there was silence again like so many of the Wrong Men in the past. So I called and demanded answers. It was a question expressed to him personally, but it could have been asked all the wrong men I had dated. I got the answer in a text message while some people were giving a vacuum cleaner demonstration at my house. He had a wife. Everything he had felt and said to me was real, but he had a wife at home waiting for him. Both his email and Twitter account had been accounts he set up solely to talk to me and he deleted them both. We never spoke again. And it left my mind wandering through the presentation knowing that it wasn't just the vacuum cleaner that sucked.

With his answer, I suddenly figured something out. When you're raised in an environment like I was, overlooked and never told that you're worth much, you truly do believe it. You will walk through your life dating the people you believe you deserve. Apparently, deep down, I felt I deserved to be treated like crap. The truth was, a lot of these Wrong Men really did have strong feelings for me. A lot of these Wrong Men were complete idiots, had no idea how to treat someone, but in the end they did love me. My "I'm unlovable" deeply-grained thinking was foiled with this realization. Things looked different and I headed out knowing that the next time I met someone, there was a very good chance he would love me as well, but I'd never put up with the crap again.

## Signs You're Dating a Man with a Secret

- Tan line on their ring finger.

- Accidently call you buy another name.

- They say they don't have a Facebook account, but you find one later with a troubling relationship status.

- You can only see them at certain times of the day, and never at their house.

# Finding Mr. Right

There's going to come a point where you no longer care about the pressure that friends or society put on you about shacking up. You'll realize the pity-filled, "Aww.. you'll find someone someday" comments stop bothering you because dating has become such a nightmare, why would you want that again? You just stop listening to advice from people in their own bad relationships about who you should date and who you should be and break out to become the person that makes you happy. It's right about then, where God might throw you a curve ball like he did with me when he introduced me to a pirate who would change everything.

I had never gone down to the Las Vegas Strip for Halloween before, so I and my Queen of Hearts costume and my friend in her Alice in Wonderland get-up headed out for the night. She told me that we had to stop by a house party on the way down. Just for a minute. I hadn't been to a house party in years, and the last time I had, drunken frat boys were screaming and spilling beer all over me. This was not something I, being at this time will into my thirties, was interested in. "OK, you get a half hour and then we're out," I told her.

We walked in through the garage, where everyone was hanging out, and within a few minutes my plans of the night completely changed. A man dressed in a pirate costume walked through the door with this huge brown hat, a smile that put the brightness of Luxor to shame and the most beautiful blue eyes I'd ever seen. That "meant to be" feeling that I hadn't felt for six years slammed into me and our eyes locked. He walked straight up to me and introduced himself. I knew two things right there. (1) This man was meant to be in my life. (2) This man had every ability to completely destroy me. For maybe a half hour we would pretend like we weren't completely gawking at each other. I would walk around talking to people when he was sitting on the couch stuck on the phone. No matter what, our eyes never left each other. It felt like we were in the middle of a conversation even from across the room. I'd roll my eyes at some guy's horrible pickup approaches and he'd point at the phone, roll his eyes back, and make that "he won't stop talking" signal with his hand.

He got off the phone and I immediately joined him on the couch. I have no idea of all the things we talked about because I was so amazed at what I was feeling. I thought of the years I had spent settling for relationships where I didn't have this feeling because I thought there was no way in a million years I'd ever feel this way again. But there it was. Suddenly he broke my escape to La La Land when he came in quickly for a kiss. Aggressive little booger! I pulled away because none of this made any sense, and I just started laughing. He said with a sly look in his eye, "Ahh.. I see how it is. You're going to make me work for it. It's cool. I got it." It got to the point where someone walked by and said, "Do we need to post a sign that says 'Reserved' for you two above that couch?" Suddenly my half hour time limit restriction on the party was extended all night.

It turned out that he didn't have to work too much harder for that first kiss, but once it happened we would have to work extremely hard to stop. As cheesy as it sounds, it felt as though our lips were genetically designed for each other's. With every single other wrong man story I had, I never felt that kissing them was as amazing as what I was experiencing with this pirate.

For the rest of the night, we'd try to interact with other people, but end up with each other again. He started talking to his friend about me in Spanish, trying to be sneaky, until I stated, "I can understand Spanish." I'd start dancing on the dance floor with my friend only to run over to him every time some other guy would try to talk to me.

It was 4:30 in the morning and the friend I came with had fallen asleep on the couch. Since I had every range of experiences at this point with men, I had no idea if I would see this guy again or if he'd just disappear from my life when I gave him my number at his car. Somehow, with his kiss on my forehead, I knew he'd be back for more. By the time I got home and plugged in my dead phone, he had already texted me to say goodnight. I was a smitten kitten in a cougar's body.

Things moved very fast with us and everything was thrown on the table upfront. We divulged all of our 'deal-breaking' info to each other within a week like we were filling an order at a McDonald's drive-through or something. "Well, due to the fact that I have dated every ass-bag in existence, I have some trust issues," I'd say. "Well, good thing I won't give you a reason to worry," he'd come back with. Somehow it all fit. It was like the scrunched up pieces of red paper were unraveling in front of me in the form of this man. The faults he was so concerned with in himself never seemed to be something to end a relationship for. They all seemed like things a couple could concur on together to me. He was too strong of a man to let my fears about getting involved with someone again destroy what was possible and he didn't let me ever go. All I could think of was what my friend's husband told my friend when they first met. "You have your shit, and I have mine… but at least we have matching baggage." This man felt right.

I knew I was falling in love with him fast, but I didn't want to jump into telling him. One night, I pulled out a piece of paper and wrote to him about how crazy it was that I was falling in love so quickly and how it just felt natural to be with him. I gave it to him and said he could open it in a year from that date. Without him opening it, I went to his house the next day. When he jumped in the car he looked at me and said, "This is ridiculous. I've never felt like this so fast in my life." He mumbled and shook his head a million times sitting there, but he eventually said, "It just feels right to say that I love you." And it was. I said I love you right back to him, and we've said it to each other every day since.

He was the biggest eye opener of my life. Ironically, he drove an Escalade, but unlike the male stripper herd at my old gym he lacked the questionable career and Sugar Momma. Any man that I had met before who had his kind of looks always used them to hook up with other women.

> He drove an Escalade, but unlike the male stripper herd at my old gym he lacked the questionable career and Sugar Momma.

He denied them at every turn. The moment I would get that old fear when I wouldn't hear from him for a while, I'd get a text saying, "Hi, Beautiful." Soon came my birthday and for the first time in a long time I held on to him tighter rather than breaking up with him as I would have done in my past. A week later came Valentine's Day, the first one I'd spend with a man in seven years, and the first one I ever felt was the true reason for the day.

My family met him and loved him, but I was past the point of caring what they thought. I was only listening to my heart. The jealousy of the only other male who mattered, my dog Kavic, subsided when he fell in love with the Pirate as well after a year of hotdog bribes. I was the person I wanted to be when I met him and he loved and encouraged exactly that. He could make me laugh at every turn by doing things like sprinting into the room to dive on top of me in bed. We could do anything together, go anywhere together, and it was like we were in our own private world. He soon became my best friend and the greatest love of my life.

This person was no wrong man. Even the first time I met his mom she told me, "He's such a sweet boy. I come home from work every day to see that he has set a bottled water out for me so I can get it on the way inside the house." Someone doing something so sweet, so consistently, could not be bad. He fought through my walls for months, and was the only man strong enough to do it. I had built up so many fears that the men I dated would criticize me, leave me, cheat on me, or take advantage of me, but each step of the way he'd greet me with understanding and slowly tear those fears away. Months later, it finally clicked that he was still there. He really was by my side. It was the first time in any relationship I finally had peace.

Neither one of us is an angel. Getting to know him, I saw many of the more ethically acceptable traits that had been deal breakers with my Wrong Men of the past. Somehow they seemed like nothing with him because the way he made me feel far outbalanced the negative. That first year, we had the issues that come up when you first start a relationship getting to know the other person's needs, but whatever the crisis, our love and dedication to each other was reason enough to fight through the problems.

Then the day came when I was sitting around with a group of girls at Happy Hour who were all talking about their husbands or boyfriends. One by one, they'd start talking about something messed up that their guy recently did. One was verbally abusive, another had been taking advantage of her for years, and the stories went on. Some had just been on a few bad dates, but several of the girls had been in relationships for years and I wondered if they had just settled at an early age with one of their Wrong Men. Finally the group looked at me and for the first time ever I said with all honesty, "I've got nothing."

The simple fact that I'm in a relationship knowing that the person I'm with truly has my best interest in mind and treats me in a way that makes my heart feel at peace, I can honestly say that I'm done dating the Wrong Men. From this point forward, my "forever" will be in a relationship feeling as this one does, or happy taking on the world alone. Either way, I have to be myself, or it's not worth it. Through my past, I know where life may take you and things might not be forever, but I sure wouldn't mind being this pirate's treasure for the long haul.

# Lessons from Dating the Wrong Men

When I was young, I had a master plan of what I thought I needed in life to be happy without even having a clue to what it was that made me content. God had that answer and a plan beyond my wildest dreams. Through each "Wrong Man," I learned the lessons of love and relationships when I was never given a map.

God was transforming me through the years and through the heartaches to become the person I needed to be to deserve the man that I mustered up on a red piece of paper so long ago. My approaches to faith, relationships, business, and life were completely different from the beginning to the end. My figure, friends, alcohol consumption, and location changed drastically, positioning me in the perfect place at the right time for my dreams as a small girl to come true.

You might be out there without direction when it comes to love. You might be in so much shock from betrayal or pain from the person you love walking out the door that you have not seen what is yet to come. You don't need to listen to that friend, parent, woman snickering about you behind your back about your dating life because chances are, the only reason they're telling you how yours should be is because they refuse to face the failures in their own. You are the person to decide if you're with the right man, no one else. When you feel that something is wrong in your heart, there is. Even if the people around you try to convince you differently, they may not know the situation completely, or they may not have your best interest in mind. If you're dating a person who tries to convince you otherwise, you're with someone who only cares about 50% of the relationship and that 50% is not you.

Even at the bottomless pit of heartache, don't ever stop living life. God may be in the process of changing you. You may find new loves in your life through travel, business, sports or art. You will develop you to be the perfect person for that perfect match or just be so happy with what you're doing, you can do it alone. No matter what, you'll develop enough good material for a book!

You might get lucky and meet the love of your life when you are five. It may be 25, 35 or 85 after having dated every jerk on the planet in between. You also might find that your ideal life lies in independence where you take on the world alone. In any approach, every princess and prince on earth is loveable. You just might need to work to surround yourself with the right family, friends, pets, bosses, divorcées, criminals, celebrities, self-proclaimed assholes, or the Right Man to remind you of the worthiness of your crown.

Share Your Wrong Man Story or Ask the Author at:

# DatingTheWrongMen.com

14.49

**LONGWOOD PUBLIC LIBRARY**
800 Middle Country Road
Middle Island, NY 11953
(631) 924-6400
longwoodlibrary.org

**LIBRARY HOURS**

| | |
|---|---|
| Monday-Friday | 9:30 a.m. - 9:00 p.m. |
| Saturday | 9:30 a.m. - 5:00 p.m. |
| Sunday (Sept-June) | 1:00 p.m. - 5:00 p.m. |

61420954R00104

Made in the USA
Lexington, KY
10 March 2017